D0988406

REVISE EDEXCEL GCSE
Religious Studies
Religion & Life (Unit 1) and Religion & Society (Unit 8) Christianity & Islam

REVISION WORKBOOK

Series Consultant: Harry Smith

Author: Tanya Hill

- -

A note from the publisher

In order to ensure that this resource offers high-quality support for the associated Edexcel qualification, it has been through a review process by the awarding body to confirm that it fully covers the teaching and learning content of the specification or part of a specification at which it is aimed, and demonstrates an appropriate balance between the development of subject skills, knowledge and understanding, in addition to preparation for assessment.

While the publishers have made every attempt to ensure that advice on the qualification and its assessment is accurate, the official specification and associated assessment guidance materials are the only authoritative source of information and should always be referred to for definitive guidance.

Edexcel examiners have not contributed to any sections in this resource relevant to examination papers for which they have responsibility.

No material from an endorsed resource will be used verbatim in any assessment set by Edexcel.

Endorsement of a resource does not mean that the resource is required to achieve this Edexcel qualification, nor does it mean that it is the only suitable material available to support the qualification, and any resource lists produced by the awarding body shall include this and other appropriate resources.

ALWAYS LEARNING

PEARSON

Contents

A small bit of small print

Edexcel publishes Sample Assessment Material and the Specification on its website. This is the official content and this book should be used in conjunction with it. The questions in this book have been written to help you practise what you have learned in your revision. Remember: the real exam questions may not look like this.

Introduction

EXAM ALERT

1 What is **agnosticism**?   **(a, 2 marks)**

....

....

....

> Students have struggled with exam questions similar to this - be prepared! **ResultsPlus**

2 What does the term **omni-benevolent** mean?   **(a, 2 marks)**

....

....

....

3 'Nobody should be an atheist.' In your answer you should refer to at least one religion.

(i) Do you agree? Give reasons for your opinion.   **(d, 3 marks)**

....

....

....

....

....

....

....

....

(ii) Give reasons why some people may disagree with you.   **(3 marks)**

....

....

....

....

> Make sure that at least one of your reasons is a religious one and try to give examples to support your reasons.

....

....

....

....

Had a go ☐   **Nearly there** ☐   **Nailed it!** ☐

Religious upbringing

1   Do you think parents should bring their children up to be religious? Give **two** reasons for your point of view.   **(b, 4 marks)**

....

....

....

....

....

....

....

> To do well on this type of (b) question, try to give two **different** reasons for your opinion.

Guided   2   'A religious upbringing is the best way to encourage belief in God.' In your answer you should refer to at least one religion.

   (i)   Do you agree? Give reasons for your opinion.   **(d, 3 marks)**

I agree with the statement because parents can teach

their children ....

....

....

....

....

....

> The question asks you to refer to at least one religion, so make sure you do this. Give your own opinion and remember to develop your reasons fully.

   (ii)   Give reasons why some people may disagree with you.   **(3 marks)**

I understand that others may disagree with me because they believe there are other

ways of knowing God such as ....

....

....

....

....

....

Religious experiences

1   What is a **religious experience**?

    (a, 2 marks)

    ....

    ....

    ....

    ....

> You need to give a short accurate explanation of the general term to achieve success in this question.

2   What does **conversion** mean?

    (a, 2 marks)

    ....

    ....

    ....

> **Guided**

3   Explain how religious experiences may lead to belief in God.

    (c, 8 marks)

    If a person had a religious experience such as seeing a
    loved one recover from illness as a result of prayer they
    might believe that ....

    ....

    ....

    ....

    ....

    ....

    ....

    ....

    ....

    ....

    ....

    ....

    ....

    ....

> Think about a conversion experience that you have studied and use it in your answer to help explain your response.

The design argument

Guided 1 Do you think science proves that God did not design the world?
Give **two** reasons for your point of view.   (b, 4 marks)

I disagree because I think there is lots of evidence to suggest that God could have

designed the world. For example ....

....

....

I also disagree because of the argument put forward by

William Paley which says ....

....

....

....

> Make sure you begin by showing that this is your own opinion.

2 Do you think that the only logical explanation for the design of the world is God?
Give **two** reasons for your point of view.   (b, 4 marks)

....

....

....

....

....

....

The causation argument

1   Do you think God is the only acceptable explanation for the cause of the universe?
Give **two** reasons for your point of view.   **(b, 4 marks)**

....

....

....

....

....

....

2   'The universe could not have happened by chance – God must have caused it.' In your
answer you should refer to at least one religion.

   (i)   Do you agree? Give reasons for your opinion.   **(d, 3 marks)**

....

....

....

....

....

....

....

....

   (ii) Give reasons why some people may disagree with you.   **(3 marks)**

....

....

....

Aim to give reasons for your
opinion, making sure you
develop your ideas.

....

....

....

....

5

The origins of the world

> **Guided** 1 Explain how Christians may respond to scientific explanations of the world.   **(c, 8 marks)**

Christians respond to scientific explanations of the origin of the world in different ways. Some Christians believe scientific explanations of the origin of the world should be rejected because ....

....

....

> Explain the different ways some Christians respond. Try to give examples.

For example, ...

....

....

....

Other Christians take a different approach arguing that science is compatible with religion and saying ....

....

....

....

> You could also explain how some Christians try to bring scientific and religious ideas about creation together.

Equally, some may argue that ....

....

....

....

Unanswered prayers

1   Do you think there is any point in praying?
Give **two** reasons for your point of view.   **(b, 4 marks)**

....

....

....

....

....

....

**EXAM
ALERT**

2   Explain why unanswered prayers may lead some people to
not believe in God.   **(c, 8 marks)**

Students have struggled with
exam questions similar to this
- be prepared! **ResultsPlus**

Remember that there are
extra marks available for the
(c) questions in Unit 1 for
QWC, so make sure you read
through your answer carefully
to check you are happy with it.

....

....

....

....

....

....

....

....

....

....

....

....

....

....

....

....

....

Had a go ☐   Nearly there ☐   Nailed it! ☐

The problem of evil and suffering

1   What is **natural evil**?   (a, 2 marks)

....

....

....

> Make sure you learn the glossary definitions.

> **Guided**   2   Do you think the presence of evil and suffering in the world proves that God does not exist?
Give **two** reasons for your point of view.   (b, 4 marks)

Although I can see why evil and suffering causes problems for belief in God, I do not agree with the statement. This is because ....

....

....

....

A second reason why I disagree with the statement is because ....

....

....

....

> You are asked for your opinion so make sure you give it and consider your reasons carefully. You should be able to support your view with evidence.

Christian responses to the problem of evil and suffering

1 What is **free will**?   (a, 2 marks)

....

....

....

> **Guided**

2 Explain how the followers of one religion respond to the problem of evil and suffering.

            (c, 8 marks)

Christians believe that evil and suffering do not cause a problem for belief in God. Some
Christians believe that evil and suffering are a test which means ....

....

....

....

Other Christians believe God created humans with free will which allows them to accept evil

and suffering because ....

....

....

....

First, think carefully about the question. You need to offer a thorough and detailed response showing how believers of **one** religion may respond in different ways to the problem that evil and suffering gives to belief in God.

Another way in which Christians respond to evil and
suffering is to follow the example of Jesus. They believe

....

....

....

Try to give as much explanation as you can and start a new paragraph for each reason.

Christians accept that they may not be able to explain the
presence of evil and suffering but believe God has a plan.
This helps them respond to the problem of evil and

suffering by ....

....

....

Finally, check through your answer, making sure that it is clear and that you have included everything you can.

Had a go ☐   **Nearly there** ☐   **Nailed it!** ☐

The media and belief in God

1   Do you think what you watch on television affects what you believe about God?
Give **two** reasons for your point of view.   **(b, 4 marks)**

....

....

....

....

....

> **Guided**

2   'The media always shows religion negatively.' In your answer you should refer to at least
one religion.

   (i)   Do you agree? Give reasons for your opinion   **(d, 3 marks)**

I agree that often religion seems to be portrayed negatively in the media. For example

....

....

....

....

....

....

   (ii) Give reasons why some people may disagree with you.   **(3 marks)**

However there are also many examples where religion is shown positively, such as ....

....

....

....

....

....

....

....

> Remember that you must
> make reference to at least one
> religion in your answer. Try to
> use examples from different
> media programmes or films
> that you have studied.

Key words

Look carefully at the key words and their definitions below – can you connect the correct key word on the left with its corresponding definition on the right?

Word

1) agnosticism

2) atheism

3) conversion

4) free will

5) miracle

6) moral evil

7) natural evil

8) numinous

9) omni-benevolent

10) omnipotent

11) omniscient

12) prayer

Definition

a) the idea that humans are free to make their own choices

b) when your life is changed by giving yourself to God

c) actions done by humans which cause suffering

d) not being sure whether God exists

e) things that cause suffering but have nothing to do with humans

f) the belief that God knows everything that has happened and everything that is going to happen

g) the belief that God is all-powerful

h) the belief that God is all-good

i) believing that God does not exist

j) an attempt to contact God, usually through words

k) the feeling of the presence of something greater than you

l) something which seems to break a law of science and makes you think only God could have done it

Christian beliefs in life after death

Guided 1 What is **resurrection**? **(a, 2 marks)**

Resurrection is the belief that..

....

....

2 'There is no life after death so you may as well enjoy your life on Earth.' In your answer you should refer to at least one religion.

   (i) Do you agree? Give reasons for your point of view. **(d, 3 marks)**

I agree with the statement because there is no evidence of
an afterlife. ....

> Think about all the evidence that suggests there is no afterlife.

....

....

....

....

....

   (ii) Give reasons why some people may disagree with your view. **(3 marks)**

Christians would disagree with my opinion because they think ....

....

....

....

....

....

....

The effect of belief in the afterlife on Christian lives

Guided 1 Explain how Christian beliefs about life after death affect the way they live their lives.

(c, 8 marks)

Belief in an afterlife will affect the way in which a Christian lives their life because ....

....

....

....

....

....

....

....

....

....

....

....

....

....

....

....

> Read the question very carefully to make sure you understand what you need to write. This is a challenging question because you need to explain the link between what a believer thinks is true and their actions.

Islamic beliefs about life after death

1 Do you think all religious believers should believe in life after death?
   Give **two** reasons for your point of view.   **(b, 4 marks)**

   ....

   ....

   ....

   ....

   ....

   ....

> **Guided** 2 'A soul is the part of a person that lives on after death.' In your answer you should refer to
       at least one religion other than Christianity.

   (i) Do you agree? Give reasons for your opinion.   **(d, 3 marks)**

   I agree/disagree because...

   ....

   ....

   ....

   I also agree/disagree because...

   ....

   ....

   ....

   ....

   (ii) Give reasons why some people may disagree with you.   **(3 marks)**

   Other people may agree/disagree* with me because ....

   ....

   ....

   Another reason why they may agree/disagree* is ....

   ....

   ....

> * Cross out the answer that
> doesn't apply to you.

Non-religious beliefs in life after death

1   What is a **near-death experience**? (a, 2 marks)

....

....

....

2   Explain why some non-religious people believe in life after death. (c, 8 marks)

....

....

....

....

....

....

....

....

....

....

....

....

....

....

....

....

....

> Remember to include some of the following ideas: death is difficult, it makes sense, near-death experiences, ghosts and reincarnation.

15

Non-belief in life after death

1   Do you think there is an afterlife?
Give **two** reasons for your point of view.   **(b, 4 marks)**

....

....

....

....

....

....

2   'Life after death is impossible.' In your answer you should refer to at least one religion.

(i)   Do you agree? Give reasons for your opinion.   **(d, 3 marks)**

....

....

....

....

....

....

....

....

(ii) Give reasons why some people may disagree with you.   **(3 marks)**

....

....

....

....

Try to include both religious
and non-religious ideas about
why there may or may not be
an afterlife.

....

....

....

....

16

Abortion

▷ **Guided** ▷   **1**   Do you think abortion is murder?
Give **two** reasons for your point of view.   **(b, 4 marks)**

I think ....

....

....

....

....

....

> Remember this question is asking for **your** opinion so make sure you can give two reasons to support what you think.

2   Explain why some people support abortion and others oppose it.   **(c, 8 marks)**

....

....

....

....

....

....

....

....

....

....

....

....

....

....

....

Christian attitudes to abortion

1   What is meant by **sanctity of life**?   **(a, 2 marks)**

....

....

....

> Think about the word special.

2   'No religious women should have an abortion.' You must refer to Christianity in your answer.

   (i)   Do you agree? Give reasons for your opinion.   **(d, 3 marks)**

....

....

....

....

....

....

....

....

   (ii)   Give reasons why someone may disagree with you.   **(3 marks)**

....

....

....

....

....

....

....

> Think about reasons why Christians support and oppose abortion. Make sure that you make your own opinion clear and use examples to support your reasons.

Muslim attitudes to abortion

Guided 1 Explain why followers of one religion other than Christianity do not agree with abortion.

(c, 8 marks)

Many Muslims do not agree with abortion because of the sanctity of life argument. This means ....

....

....

....

> Remember to **explain fully** why Muslims do not accept abortion. The most successful answers are those that give relevant reasons supported by examples and show awareness of different views and why they are held.

Muslim beliefs about the soul also affect their views about abortion. This is because ....

....

....

....

Many Muslims will view abortion as the deliberate ending of a life which they consider to be wrong because...

....

....

....

> Give as many reasons as possible to explain Muslim views, making sure you develop the key ideas.

Finally, ...

....

....

....

....

Euthanasia

1 What is **voluntary euthanasia**? (a, 2 marks)

....

....

....

Guided 2 Do you think euthanasia is always wrong?
Give **two** reasons for your point of view. (b, 4 marks)

I believe that euthanasia is always wrong. One reason for my

view is that ....

....

....

....

A second reason for my view is that ....

....

....

....

> Remember that you must give **two** different reasons for your opinion to be successful. Giving an example for each reason is a good way to develop your answers.

Christian attitudes to euthanasia

1   Do you think Christians should always oppose euthanasia?
    Give **two** reasons for your point of view.   **(b, 4 marks)**

    ....

    ....

    ....

    ....

    ....

    ....

⟩**Guided**⟩   2   'The UK's law on euthanasia should be changed.' In your answer you should refer to at
    least one religion.

    (i) Do you agree? Give reasons for your view.   **(d, 3 marks)**

    I agree/disagree because ....

    ....

    ....

    I also agree/disagree because ....

    ....

    ....

    Finally ....

    ....

    ....

    ....

> Remember to think carefully
> about whether you agree
> or disagree with the given
> statement as you must be able
> to support it with evidence
> and reasons for your view.

    (ii) Give reasons why some people may disagree with you.   **(3 marks)**

    Other people may disagree with me because ....

    ....

    ....

    ....

    ....

    ....

    ....

    ....

> Remember that you must
> make reference to at least one
> religion in your answer. Try to
> offer at least **three** reasons for
> your view. You could include
> some reasons from both
> Christianity and Islam in your
> response.

Muslim attitudes to euthanasia

1   Do you think religious people should always oppose euthanasia?
Give **two** reasons for your point of view.   **(b, 4 marks)**

....

....

....

....

....

....

....

> Try to answer this question from an Islamic point of view

Guided ▷ 2   Choose one religion other than Christianity and explain why some of its followers accept euthanasia and others do not.   **(c, 8 marks)**

Muslims believe euthanasia is wrong for many reasons. One reason for this is due to their beliefs about the sanctity of life ....

....

....

A second reason concerns their beliefs about Allah because ....

....

....

....

Muslims also believe that they have a duty to care for the sick and elderly. This makes euthanasia wrong because ....

....

....

....

However, some Muslims may accept that ....

....

....

....

....

> Make sure you read the question carefully. This question asks you to think about an issue from both sides, other questions might only want you to explain one point of view. Think about including some of the following reasons: human life is sacred, it is Allah's choice, it is like murder, suffering is a test, and all human life is valuable.

Matters of life and death in the media

Guided 1 Do you think the media should be allowed to report on matters of life and death? Give **two** reasons for your point of view. **(b, 4 marks)**

I think that issues of abortion and euthanasia are important and therefore the media should be allowed to report on them. This is because ....

....

....

I also think the media should be allowed to report on these issues because the media should not shy away from difficult issues. Because ....

....

....

2 'The media should not be allowed to criticise religious ideas about matters of life and death.' You should refer to at least one religion in your answer.

(i) Do you agree? Give reasons for your opinion. **(d, 3 marks)**

....

....

....

....

....

....

....

....

(ii) Give reasons why some may disagree with you. **(3 marks)**

....

....

....

....

....

....

....

Key words

Look carefully at the key words and their definitions below – can you connect the correct key word on the left with its corresponding definition on the right?

Word	Definition
1) abortion	a) the idea that the soul lives on after the death of the body
2) assisted suicide	b) ending someone's life painlessly when they are unable to ask, but you have good reason for thinking they would want you to do so
3) euthanasia	c) the idea that life must have some benefits for it to be worth living
4) immortality of the soul	d) providing a seriously ill person with the means to commit suicide
5) near-death experience	e) the belief that, after death, the body stays in the grave until the end of the world when it is raised
6) non-voluntary euthanasia	f) ending life painlessly when someone in great pain asks for death
7) paranormal	g) unexplained things which are thought to have spiritual causes, for example ghosts, mediums
8) quality of life	h) the belief that, after death, souls are reborn into a new body
9) reincarnation	i) the removal of a foetus from the womb before it can survive
10) resurrection	j) the belief that life is holy and belongs to God
11) sanctity of life	k) when someone about to die has an out of body experience
12) voluntary euthanasia	l) the painless killing of someone dying from a painful disease

Changing attitudes towards marriage and the family in the UK

1 What is a **nuclear family**? *(a, 2 marks)*

....

....

....

2 What is a **re-constituted family**? *(a, 2 marks)*

....

....

....

....

> Remember that you need to give a short accurate definition to do well on these questions

Guided **3** Explain how family life has changed in the UK. *(c, 8 marks)*

Family life has changed today because of ....

....

....

....

....

....

....

....

> Consider the changes that have happened in attitudes towards marriage, divorce and homosexuality to explain why families have changed so much.

There are many different types of families today whereas
there traditionally only used to be one. Today we have ....

....

....

....

....

....

....

> Explain your points in as much depth as you can. Try to include an example to support each point. **Remember, you can make up to four points.**

Christian attitudes to sex outside marriage

1 Do you think sex outside marriage is acceptable?
Give **two** reasons for your point of view.   **(b, 4 marks)**

....

....

....

....

....

....

....

> Remember, sex outside of marriage can include reference to sex before marriage as well as adultery. Make sure you make clear that this is your opinion and give an example to support each of your two reasons.

Guided 2 'Christian ideas about sex outside marriage are out of date today.' In your answer you should refer to at least one religion.

(i) Do you agree? Give reasons for your opinion.   **(d, 3 marks)**

I agree with the statement because ideas about sex and marriage have changed. Today

....

....

....

....

....

....

....

(ii) Give reasons why some people may disagree with you.   **(3 marks)**

Most Christians would probably disagree with me because they believe ....

....

....

....

....

....

> You are asked to give your opinion and reasons for this view. Then you need to show awareness of the conflicting view. Try to explain yourself clearly and keep the two sides of your answer separate.

Muslim attitudes to sex outside marriage

> **Guided**   **1**   Choose one religion other than Christianity and explain what its followers believe about sex outside marriage.   **(c, 8 marks)**

All Muslims believe that sex outside marriage is wrong and forbidden. One reason why they think this is because sex is special and ....

....

| The most successful answers offer reasons that are well explained and developed. |

A second reason why Muslims hold this view is because they think that the purpose of sex is to have children and therefore sex outside marriage ....

....

....

The Qur'an teaches sex outside marriage is wrong and Muslims ....

....

....

Muslims believe that adultery or cheating is wrong because marriage is intended ....

....

....

> **Guided**   **2**   'Religious teachings about sex outside marriage are out of date in today's society.' In your answer you should refer to at least one religion.

(i)   Do you agree? Give reasons for your opinion.   **(d, 3 marks)**

I agree with the statement because I believe ideas about sex and marriage have changed. ....

....

....

....

(ii)   Give reasons why some people may disagree with you.   **(3 marks)**

Muslims would disagree with me because Islam teaches that ....

....

....

....

....

Christian attitudes to divorce

1   What is meant by **faithfulness**?   **(a, 2 marks)**

   ....

   ....

   ....

2   'Divorce is always wrong.' In your answer you should refer to at least one religion.

   (i)   Do you agree? Give reasons for your opinion.   **(d, 3 marks)**

   ....

   ....

   ....

   ....

   ....

   ....

   ....

   ....

> It is helpful when you have questions like this to quickly plan out what you need to include. Think about the reasons why people agree and disagree about divorce that you have studied in class.

   (ii) Give reasons why some people may disagree with you.   **(3 marks)**

   ....

   ....

   ....

   ....

   ....

   ....

   ....

   ....

   ....

Muslim attitudes to divorce

Guided 1 Do you think divorce is ever right?
Give **two** reasons for your point of view.   **(b, 4 marks)**

I agree / disagree because ....

....

....

....

A second reason why I think this is because ....

....

....

> Make it clear that this is your opinion and make sure you give **two** well thought out reasons to support your view. Cross out the answer that doesn't apply to you.

2 'All religious believers should allow divorce.' In your answer you should refer to one religion other than Christianity.

   (i) Do you agree? Give reasons for your opinion.   **(d, 3 marks)**

....

....

....

....

....

....

....

....

   (ii) Give reasons why some people may disagree with you.   **(3 marks)**

....

....

....

....

....

....

....

Christian teachings on family life

1 Explain what is meant by a **reconstituted family**. (a, 2 marks)

....

....

....

Guided 2 Explain why Christians believe family life is important. (c, 8 marks)

Christians believe the family is very important. It is where children are taught about ....

....

....

....

> With a question such as this, it helps to start a new paragraph for each idea and try to offer a full explanation, using relevant examples.

Another reason why the family is important is because of the community offered by Christianity. This means ....

....

....

The Bible contains important teachings about the family such as ....

....

....

....

Finally, children brought up in a Christian family can attend Sunday school where they can ......

....

....

....

Muslim teachings on family life

1   What is an **extended family**?   **(a, 2 marks)**

....

....

....

> Make sure you learn the key words for each section thoroughly.

> **Guided**

2   Do you think a religious family is the best type of family to raise children?
   Give **two** reasons for your point of view.   **(b, 4 marks)**

I think that the religious family is / isn't* the best environment for children to be brought up in. One reason for my view is that ....

....

....

....

A second reason for my view is that ....

....

....

....

> * Cross out the answer that doesn't apply to you

> Remember that the most successful candidates develop their ideas. Here you could explain Muslim beliefs about the importance of family and what is provided by the family.

> You could give an example to support each point you make.

Christian attitudes to homosexuality

1   Do you think all religious people should accept homosexuality?
Give **two** reasons for your point of view.   **(b, 4 marks)**

....

....

....

....

....

....

....

> Remember that you must be able to give **two** reasons to support your opinion.

2   Do you think religious teachings about homosexuality are out of date today?
Give **two** reasons for your point of view.   **(b, 4 marks)**

....

....

....

....

....

....

Muslim attitudes to homosexuality

1   What is **homosexuality**?   **(a, 2 marks)**

....

....

....

2   'No religious person should be homosexual.' In your answer you should refer to at least
    one religion.   **(d, 3 marks)**

   (i)   Do you agree? Give reasons for your opinion.

   ....

   ....

   ....

   ....

   ....

   ....

   ....

   ....

   (ii) Give reasons why some people may disagree with you.   **(3 marks)**

   ....

   ....

   ....

   ....

   ....

   ....

   ....

   ....

   ....

> You could try to make
> reference to Islam and
> Islamic teachings in a
> question such as this
> because most Muslims
> hold such strong views
> against homosexuality.

Christian attitudes to contraception

1 'Contraception should be accepted by all religious people.' In your answer you should refer to at least one religion.

    (i) Do you agree? Give reasons for your opinion.   **(d, 3 marks)**

    ....

    ....

    ....

    ....

> Make sure you take time to really understand the statement so that you can answer the question properly.

....

....

....

....

....

    (ii) Give reasons why some people may disagree with you.   **(3 marks)**

    ....

    ....

    ....

    ....

> Remember to show in your answers that you understand that different religious believers hold different views on issues such as contraception.

    ....

....

....

....

....

Muslim attitudes to contraception

1 What is **procreation**?   **(a, 2 marks)**

....

....

....

2 'Contraception is against the will of God.' In your answer you should refer to at least one religion.

(i) Do you agree? Give reasons for your opinion.   **(d, 3 marks)**

....

....

....

....

....

....

....

....

(ii) Give reasons why some people may disagree with you.   **(3 marks)**

....

....

....

....

....

....

....

....

....

> Remember that you must make reference to at least one religion in your answer. You could try and include Islamic teachings on contraception because there is some variation in what different Muslims think.

Key words

Look carefully at the key words and their definitions below – can you connect the correct key word on the left with its corresponding definition on the right?

Word

1) adultery
2) civil partnership
3) cohabitation
4) contraception
5) faithfulness
6) homosexuality
7) nuclear family
8) pre-marital sex
9) procreation
10) promiscuity
11) re-constituted family
12) re-marriage

Definition

a) staying with your marriage partner and having sex only with them
b) sexual attraction to the same sex
c) living together without being married
d) a sexual act between a married person and someone other than their marriage partner
e) where two sets of children (stepbrothers and stepsisters) become one family when their divorced parents marry each other
f) mother, father and children living as a unit
g) making a new life
h) marrying again after being divorced from a previous marriage
i) having sex with a number of partners without commitment
j) sex before marriage
k) intentionally preventing pregnancy from occurring
l) a legal ceremony giving a homosexual couple the same legal rights as a husband and wife

Changing attitudes to gender roles in the UK

1 What is **prejudice**?   **(a, 2 marks)**

....

....

....

....

> Questions 1 and 2: successful answers try to offer an accurate and well-explained definition of the terms. Remember one of these is an **opinion** and the other is an **action**.

2 What is a **discrimination**?   **(a, 2 marks)**

....

....

....

3 'Men and women are still not treated equally in the UK today.' In your answer you should refer to at least one religion.

  (i) Do you agree? Give reasons for your opinion.   **(d, 3 marks)**

....

....

....

....

....

....

....

> Give your opinion about the statement, and try to offer at least **three** reasons for your view. At least **one** of your reasons for the whole answer should be a religious one.

  (ii) Give reasons why some people may disagree with you.   **(3 marks)**

....

....

....

....

....

....

....

Christian attitudes to equal rights for women in religion

1   Do you think men and women will ever be equal in Christianity?
     Give **two** reasons for your point of view.   (b, 4 marks)

....

....

....

....

....

....

> Guided   2   Explain why some Christians support equal rights for women in religion and why some do
>   not.   (c, 8 marks)

Some Christians believe women should have equal rights to
men in religion because the Bible teaches that God created
men and women as equal. It says ....

....

....

Another reason why they may suggest that women should
be treated equally to men within religion is because of the
way Jesus treated women. Through his actions he showed ....

....

....

Some Christians also have women priests because ....

....

....

....

Other Christians, however, use the story of Adam and Eve in the Bible to suggest women
are inferior to men. They argue ....

....

....

Some Christians may suggest that women cannot take the role of a priest because ....

....

> It is important that you take
> time to read the question as
> these (c) questions do not
> always require the same sort
> of answer. Here, for example,
> you are asked to write about
> **both** sides of this argument,
> **not** just one.

Muslim attitudes to equal rights for women in religion

Guided 1 Choose one religion other than Christianity and explain why some of its followers do not accept women leaders in religion. **(c, 8 marks)**

Some followers of Islam do not accept women leaders in

religion because ....

....

....

....

> Think about what the Qur'an says about men and women to explain why some Muslims do not accept women leaders.

They also feel that women ....

....

....

....

Finally, the Qur'an shows that ....

....

....

....

....

....

....

....

The UK as a multi-ethnic society

1 What is a **multi-ethnic society**? **(a, 2 marks)**

....

....

....

> Students have struggled with exam questions similar to this - be prepared! **ResultsPlus**

2 What is meant by **racial harmony**? **(a, 2 marks)**

....

....

....

3 Do you think the UK is a successful multi-ethnic society? Give **two** reasons for your point of view. **(b, 4 marks)**

....

....

....

....

> When offering your reasons to agree or disagree with the question, try to give examples to illustrate your opinion.

....

....

....

Government action to promote community cohesion

1   Do you think the action taken by the government to promote community cohesion in the UK has been successful?
Give **two** reasons for your point of view.   **(b, 4 marks)**

....

....

....

....

....

....

2   'It does not matter what action the government takes to promote community cohesion; racism will always exist.' In your answer you should refer to at least one religion.

(i)   Do you agree? Give reasons for your opinion.   **(d, 3 marks)**

....

....

....

....

....

....

....

....

(ii) Give reasons why some people may disagree with you.   **(3 marks)**

....

....

....

....

....

....

....

> Success in these questions depends on you thinking about reasons to agree **and** disagree with the given statement. Make sure that the two sides are clearly separated in your answer. Also remember that you must refer to ideas from at least one religion.

Had a go ☐   Nearly there ☐   Nailed it! ☐

Why Christians should promote racial harmony

Guided 1 Explain why it is important for Christians to promote racial harmony.   **(c, 8 marks)**

Christians believe racial harmony is important. The Bible
teaches that ....

....

....

....

....

Another reason why racial harmony is important is because Jesus ....

....

....

....

There are many examples of Christians who have stood up to try and achieve racial harmony
such as Martin Luther King. He was a ....

....

Finally, today the Church of England has its own Race and Community Relations Committee
which shows ....

....

....

> Try to give more than **one**
> reason and back up your
> answer with examples and
> evidence. Remember to make
> sure that you use the key
> words correctly and check
> your answer thoroughly as
> there are marks available for
> QWC on these questions.

2 Do you think religious people should do more to promote racial harmony?
   Give **two** reasons for your point of view.   **(b, 4 marks)**

....

....

....

....

....

....

Why Muslims should promote racial harmony

> **Guided** 1 'Religion does not help racial harmony.' In your answer you should refer to at least one religion.

(i) Do you agree? Give reasons for your opinion.   **(d, 3 marks)**

I agree with the statement because I believe that religion causes differences and therefore problems between people. An example of this is ....

....

....

A second reason for my view is ....

....

....

....

(ii) Give reasons why some people may disagree with you.   **(3 marks)**

I think Muslims would disagree with my opinion. They work to try and achieve racial harmony. Actions such as all Muslims praying together ....

....

....

The Qur'anic teachings also show that Muslims would disagree with my opinion because ....

....

| You could try to think of a third reason for each side of the debate. |

....

....

....

....

| Next, you could try and answer this question from the opposite point of view. |

43

Had a go ☐   Nearly there ☐   Nailed it! ☐

The UK as a multi-faith society

1   What is meant by **religious freedom**?   (a, 2 marks)

   ....

   ....

   ....

2   Do you think it is good for religious people to live in a multi-faith society?
   Give **two** reasons for your point of view.   (b, 4 marks)

   ....

   ....

   ....

   ....

   ....

   ....

3   'Multi-faith societies are better for religious people.' In your answer you should refer to at
   least one religion.

   (i)   Do you agree? Give reasons for your opinion.   (d, 3 marks)

   ....

   ....

   ....

   ....

   ....

   ....

   ....

   (ii) Give reasons why some people may disagree with you.   (3 marks)

   ....

   ....

   ....

   ....

   ....

   ....

> Perhaps you could try making a list of the benefits and challenges to a multi-faith society. Then think about which reasons reflect your opinion. Also consider what different religious believers would argue and why.

Issues raised about multi-faith societies

1   What is **religious pluralism**?   **(a, 2 marks)**

....

....

....

2   Do you think it is difficult to bring up religious children in a multi-faith society?
Give **two** reasons for your point of view.   **(b, 4 marks)**

....

....

....

....

....

....

....

....

> When offering your opinion on this idea, consider carefully the benefits and challenges to living in a multi-faith society. The question tells you to give **two** reasons for your opinion, so make sure you do!

> Begin your answer by making clear that this is your opinion.

Had a go ☐   Nearly there ☐   Nailed it! ☐

Religion and community cohesion

1   Do you think religions can do more to promote community cohesion? Give **two** reasons for your point of view.   **(b, 4 marks)**

....

....

....

....

....

....

〉**Guided**〉   2   Explain how religions promote community cohesion in the UK.   **(c, 8 marks)**

To try and achieve community cohesion, religious believers

have ....

....

....

....

| Think carefully about how you will answer this question because it is worth 8 marks. Spend time answering it and making sure that you know what the question asks. |

Through religious groups such as ....

....

| Try to build your answer up, giving as many reasons and examples as you can. |

....

....

....

They also ....

....

....

....

One successful example of community cohesion is ....

....

....

....

Issues of religion and community cohesion in the media

1 What is **racism**? (a, 2 marks)

....

....

....

2 Do you think the media presents a positive view of community cohesion?
Give **two** reasons for your point of view. (b, 4 marks)

....

....

....

....

....

....

....

> Make sure you read the question carefully. This question is asking about two key ideas – the media and community cohesion. You must make sure your answer reflects this.

Key words

Look carefully at the key words and their definitions below – can you connect the correct key word on the left with its corresponding definition on the right?

Word

Definition

Word	Definition
1) community cohesion	a) treating people less favourably because of their ethnicity / gender / colour / sexuality / age / class
2) discrimination	b) marriage where the husband and wife are from different religions
3) ethnic minority	c) believing some people are inferior or superior without even knowing them
4) interfaith marriages	d) the belief that some races are superior to others
5) multi-ethnic society	e) discriminating against people because of their gender (being male or female)
6) multi-faith society	f) many different races and cultures living together in one society
7) prejudice	g) a member of an ethnic group (race) which is much smaller than the majority group
8) racial harmony	h) many different religions living together in one society
9) racism	i) accepting all religions as having an equal right to coexist
10) religious freedom	j) different races / colours living together happily
11) religious pluralism	k) a common vision and shared sense of belonging for all groups in society
12) sexism	l) the right to practise your religion and change your religion

Exam skills: (a) questions and SPaG

Guided ⟩   **1**   What does **omniscient** mean?   **(a, 2 marks)**

Omniscient is a word used to describe God.

To be successful in this question, you need to offer a short but accurate definition of the term given. In this case, the student realises that the word **omniscient** is associated with God but they have not actually explained what the term means.
Can you add **one** more sentence giving an accurate definition of the term?

....

....

....

Spelling, punctuation and grammar

There are extra marks you can earn in Section 1 of the Unit 1 exam paper for Spelling, Punctuation and Grammar (SPaG). To be successful here, your spelling, punctuation and grammar need to be really good in all your answers. You need to use these to help make what you want to say very clear. Try to also use a good range of key words accurately.

Try and answer the question below, thinking particularly about your spelling, punctuation and grammar.

Guided ⟩   **2**   Do you think everyone should believe in God?
Give **two** reasons for your point of view.   **(b, 4 marks)**

I .... that everyone should believe in God. One reason for my opinion is ....

....

....

A second reason for my opinion is that ....

....

....

....

Exam skills: (b) questions

1   Do you think science explains how the world was created?
Give **two** reasons for your point of view.   **(b, 4 marks)**

> I disagree because I think that science tells us about many things but it does not explain everything. It does not tell us for example what caused the Big Bang or how the world is so perfect.

> The answer given by the student offers their opinion but only one reason for their view. The question clearly states that you must offer **two** reasons. To improve this answer you would need to think about a second reason why you would disagree that science explains how the world was created. You would also need to develop the second reason like the first. This can be done by giving an example.

> Now, see whether you can write the answer from the **opposite** point of view. Think about the tips given above.

Guided   2   Do you think science explains how the world was created?
Give **two** reasons for your point of view.   **(b, 4 marks)**

I agree that science explains how the world was created. ....

....

....

....

....

....

....

Exam skills: (c) questions

> **Guided**

1   Explain why some Christians agree with the use of contraception and others do not.

(c, 8 marks)

> Some Christians such as Roman Catholics believe that the purpose of sex is to have children and be able to start a family. They think that every sexual act between a married couple should be open to the possibility of children and that contraception stops this and is wrong.
>
> Some Christians will also argue that the use of contraception has led to promiscuity where people have sex with a number of partners without commitment.
>
> Other Christians however believe that the use of contraception for the right reasons is acceptable.

> This answer shows some understanding of the different Christian attitudes to contraception but the points made are not fully explained or just describe rather than explaining.
>
> To improve this answer, you need to develop the reasons why some Christians may **accept** certain forms of contraception and others **do not**. This means adding further explanation. You could include some reference to religious teaching in the Bible or give examples. You could also think about which types of contraception are acceptable and which are not.

> Can you improve the answer in the space below?

....

....

....

....

....

....

....

....

....

....

....

....

> Remember that in every (c) question in the Unit 1 paper, you will also be assessed on the quality of your written communication (QWC). This means you need to make sure that what you want to say is well organised and very clear. Try to also use any key words accurately. Go back over your finished answer and check that you're happy with all these points.

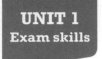

Exam skills: (d) questions

> **Guided**

1 'All religious believers should try to convert others to their religion.' In your answer you should refer to at least one religion.

(i) Do you agree? Give reasons for your opinion.   **(d, 3 marks)**

> I disagree strongly with the idea that religious believers should try to convert others to their religion. I do not believe that anyone has the right to try and convince others to do the same as them. If it were just sharing their faith that would be okay but trying to make people become religious is wrong.

(ii) Give reasons why some people might disagree with you.   **(3 marks)**

> I think some people would disagree with me because their faith tells them to.

The student has given their opinion but only offered one reason for their view, which is not developed. This answer would also benefit from having up to two more reasons included to explain why they disagree with the statement.

The second part of the answer could be improved by indicating which type of religious believers are being mentioned. It could be developed by explaining that some followers believe they have a duty to share their faith with others and try to convert them. Again, the answer would benefit from up to two more reasons.

Now try to improve the answer in the space below.

(i) ....

....

....

....

....

....

....

....

(ii) ....

....

....

....

....

....

....

Christians and the Bible

1   What is **the decalogue**?   (a, 2 marks)

....

....

⟩Guided⟩   2   Explain why some Christians use only the Bible when making moral decisions and some
do not.   (c, 8 marks)

The authority of the Bible is important to Christians because ....

....

When making moral decisions, some Christians choose to only refer to the Bible. This is

because ....

....

....

Secondly, ...

....

....

....

Other Christians choose to use other sources of authority such as ....

....

This is because they believe ....

....

....

Also, ...

....

....

....

Christians and the authority of the Church

1   What is meant by **the Church**?   **(a, 2 marks)**

....

....

....

> Don't forget that '**the Church**' and '**church**' have different meanings.

2   'There are better sources of authority for a Christian than the Church.' In your answer you should refer to Christianity.

   (i)   Do you agree? Give reasons for your opinion.   **(d, 3 marks)**

....

....

....

....

....

....

....

....

   (ii) Give reasons why some people might disagree with you.   **(3 marks)**

....

....

....

....

....

....

....

....

....

Christians and conscience

> Guided

1 Explain why some Christians believe they should follow their conscience when making moral decisions.   **(c, 8 marks)**

Some Christians believe it is important to use the conscience when making moral decisions

because ....

....

....

....

An example of when a Christian might especially rely on their conscience is ....

....

....

....

Also, ...

....

....

....

Finally ....

....

....

....

Consider the advantages of using the conscience as well as what Christians teach about the conscience. Try to use a new paragraph for each point you make so that you can easily check that your answer is clear.

Had a go ☐   Nearly there ☐   Nailed it! ☐

Christians and Situation Ethics

1   What is **Situation Ethics**?   (a, 2 marks)

....

....

....

2   What is the **Golden Rule**?   (a, 2 marks)

....

....

....

3   Do you think it is always possible to apply the Golden Rule today?
      Give **two** reasons for your point of view.   (b, 4 marks)

....

....

....

....

....

....

....

....

> Remember that you must offer your own opinion in this question. You could give examples to support what you are trying to say.

Christians and the variety of moral authorities

1   What is a **pressure group**?   **(a, 2 marks)**

....

....

....

Guided   2   Explain why Christians may use a variety of sources of authority when making moral decisions.   **(c, 8 marks)**

Christians believe it is important to do what God wants when making moral decisions. The reason some Christians will refer to a range of sources of authority is because ....

....

....

....

....

....

....

....

> Make sure you try to explain what different sources of authorities Christians can refer to and why they might choose to rely on a combination. Try to give a number of well-developed reasons to support your points. The fewer reasons you give, the more you need to explain your answer.

....

....

....

....

....

....

....

....

Human rights in the UK

Guided

1   Do you think it is always right to put human rights above everything else?
Give **two** reasons for your point of view.   **(b, 4 marks)**

I think ....

....

....

....

A second reason for my view is ....

....

....

> Students have struggled with exam questions similar to this – be prepared! **ResultsPlus**

> You could try to think of examples that have caused people to disagree about whether it is right or not to uphold human rights.

2   'Everyone is entitled to their human rights.' You should refer to Christianity in your answer.

   (i) Do you agree? Give reasons for your opinion.   **(d, 3 marks)**

....

....

....

....

....

....

....

....

> In your answer, at least one of your reasons should be a religious one. Give your own opinion in the first part of the answer and make sure you separate reasons why others may disagree and put these in the second part.

   (ii) Give reasons why some people might disagree with you.   **(3 marks)**

....

....

....

....

....

....

....

....

Why human rights are important to Christians

1   Do you think everyone is entitled to the same human rights?
Give **two** reasons for your point of view.   **(b, 4 marks)**

....

....

....

....

....

....

> **Guided**   2   'Christians should always support human rights.' You should refer to Christianity in your answer.

(i) Do you agree? Give reasons for your opinion.   **(d, 3 marks)**

I agree that Christians should always support human rights because ....

....

....

Also, Christians think all humans are equal and therefore

| You could try and give a third reason here too |

....

....

....

....

(ii) Give reasons why some people may disagree with you.   **(3 marks)**

However, some people may disagree and argue that human rights is nothing to do with

religion and ....

....

....

Another reason is ....

....

....

Also, ...

....

The importance of democratic and electoral processes

1   What is meant by **democratic process**?   **(a, 2 marks)**

....

....

....

2   What is meant by **a political party**?   **(a, 2 marks)**

....

....

....

3   Explain why it is important to vote in elections.   **(c, 8 marks)**

....

....

....

....

....

....

| Try to show that you really understand why it is important to vote in elections and give examples to support your answer. Think carefully about what the question is asking and perhaps plan your answer first. |

....

....

....

....

....

....

....

....

....

Christian teachings on moral duties and responsibilities

1 Do you think we should always treat others the way we want to be treated?
   Give **two** reasons for your point of view.   **(b, 4 marks)**

   ....

   ....

   ....

   ....

   ....

   ....

2 Explain why Christians believe they have a moral duty to help others.   **(c, 8 marks)**

   ....

   ....

   ....

   ....

   ....

> Make sure you actually explain the reasons why Christians believe they have a moral duty to help others. Try not to just list arguments but explain them using words like 'because.'

   ....

   ....

   ....

   ....

   ....

   ....

   ....

   ....

   ....

   ....

The nature of genetic engineering

 1   Explain why some people think genetic engineering is a good idea and some do not.

(c, 8 marks)

Some people may agree with genetic engineering because

....

....

....

....

....

....

....

....

> Make sure you read the question carefully. This question asks you to explain **two** sides of a debate, not just one. So make sure you do this! Also, it doesn't require you to give a religious answer, although you could use religion to explain why some people do or do not agree.

> Try to give as many reasons for your explanation as you can but remember that the fewer reasons you give, the more well developed they must be.

Some people may disagree with genetic engineering because ....

....

....

....

....

....

....

....

....

2   Do you agree with cloning?
Give **two** reasons for your point of view.

(b, 4 marks)

....

....

....

....

....

....

Christian attitudes to genetic engineering

1 Do you think genetic engineering is a good thing?
   Give **two** reasons for your point of view.   **(b, 4 marks)**

   ....

   ....

   ....

   ....

   ....

   ....

2 'Christians should always support genetic engineering.' In your answer you should refer
   to at least one religion.

   (i) Do you agree? Give reasons for your opinion.   **(d, 3 marks)**

   ....

   ....

   ....

   ....

   ....

   ....

   ....

   ....

   (ii) Give reasons why some people may disagree with you.   **(3 marks)**

   ....

   ....

   ....

   ....

   ....

   ....

   ....

   ....

   > Remember to think carefully
   > about the reasons why
   > Christians may support or
   > oppose genetic engineering.
   > Clearly give your opinion
   > and try to show that you
   > understand why people might
   > have these views and whether
   > you agree with them or not.

Key words

Look carefully at the key words and their definitions below – can you connect the correct key word on the left with its corresponding definition on the right?

Word

1) Bible

2) Church

3) conscience

4) the Decalogue

5) democratic processes

6) electoral processes

7) the Golden Rule

8) human rights

9) political party

10) pressure group

11) Situation Ethics

12) social change

Definition

a) the Ten Commandments

b) a group which tries to be elected into power on the basis of its policies (e.g. Labour, Conservative)

c) the holy book of Christians

d) the ways in which voting is organised

e) the idea that Christians should base moral decisions on what is the most loving thing to do

f) the community of Christians (with a small 'c' it means a Christian place of worship)

g) the way in which society has changed and is changing (and also the possibilities for future change)

h) a group formed to influence government policy on a particular issue

i) an inner feeling of the rightness or wrongness of an action

j) the rights and freedoms to which everyone is entitled

k) the teaching of Jesus that you should treat others as you would like them to treat you

l) the ways in which all citizens can take part in government (usually through elections)

Global warming

1   Do you think we can do more to stop global warming?
    Give **two** reasons for your point of view.   **(b, 4 marks)**

    ....

    ....

    ....

    ....

    ....

    ....

    ....

> Remember that you are asked to give **two** reasons to answer this question.

2   Explain the possible solutions to global warming.   **(c, 8 marks)**

    ....

    ....

    ....

    ....

    ....

    ....

    ....

    ....

    ....

    ....

    ....

    ....

    ....

    ....

    ....

    ....

    ....

> Try to give up to four possible solutions. You can use phrases such as 'because' to help you explain and you can try to develop your answer using examples where appropriate.

Pollution

Guided **1** Explain how people could reduce pollution.   **(c, 8 marks)**

To try to overcome the problems caused by pollution,
people could create less waste by ....

....

....

....

....

They could also lobby the government to ....

....

....

Something else people could do is ....

....

....

....

Finally, they could ....

....

....

....

> Try to build up your answer offering different ideas of things that could be done, explaining each one thoroughly.

66

Natural resources

1   What is meant by **conservation**?   **(a, 2 marks)**

....

....

....

....

> Remember to learn your key words thoroughly

> **Guided**

2   Do you think we should use more renewable resources?
Give **two** reasons for your point of view.   **(b, 4 marks)**

I .... that humans should use more renewable resources today because

....

....

....

....

Also, ...

....

....

> Begin by stating whether you agree or disagree.

> Read the question carefully. This question is asking you to consider the benefits of **renewable** resources rather than those that are not renewable.

Christian teachings on stewardship and attitudes to the environment

1 What is **stewardship**? **(a, 2 marks)**

....

....

2 What is meant by **the environment**? **(a, 2 marks)**

....

....

 3 'Christians should care for the world rather than caring for other people.' You should refer to at least one religion in your answer.

(i) Do you agree? Give reasons for your opinion. **(d, 3 marks)**

I disagree with this statement because humans were made according to Christianity in

'God's image.' This means ....

....

A second reason for my opinion is because

....

....

....

....

> You should give up to three reasons for your opinion. Can you think of another to add here?

(ii) Give reasons why some people may disagree with you. **(3 marks)**

Some Christians may disagree with my view because ....

....

Although Christians believe that humans are important, they may suggest that without the world, humans couldn't live anyway so ....

> Remember at least one of your reasons should be a religious one.

....

....

....

....

Muslim teachings on stewardship and attitudes to the environment

1   Do you think all religious believers should help care for the environment?
    Give **two** reasons for your point of view.   (b, 4 marks)

....

....

....

....

| Remember that this question is asking for your opinion so give it, for example 'I think that….' Perhaps think about answering this with Islam in mind. |

....

....

2   Choose one religion other than Christianity and explain why its followers believe it is
    important to care for the environment.   (c, 8 marks)

....

....

....

....

....

....

....

....

....

....

....

....

....

....

....

Medical treatment for infertility

1 What is an **embryo**? **(a, 2 marks)**

....

....

....

2 What is meant by **in-vitro fertilisation**? **(a, 2 marks)**

....

....

....

> Try to offer a short but accurate explanation of each term.

Guided

3 'Money on infertility treatment could be better spent elsewhere.' In your answer you should refer to at least one religion.

(i) Do you agree? Give reasons for your point of view. **(d, 3 marks)**

I .... with the statement because

....

....

> Make it clear whether you agree or disagree with the statement and try to give at least one religious reason.

Secondly, ...

....

....

I also think that ....

....

(ii) Give reasons why some people may disagree with you. **(3 marks)**

Some people may disagree with my opinion because

....

> Make it clear why others might agree or disagree with you.

Also, ...

....

....

Finally, ...

....

....

Christian attitudes to fertility treatments

1   'Christians should always seek medical treatment if facing infertility issues.' In your answer you should refer to at least one religion.

(i)   Do you agree? Give reasons for your opinion.   **(d, 3 marks)**

....

....

....

> Make sure you read the statement carefully so that you can respond to it correctly.

....

....

....

....

....

(ii) Give reasons why some people may disagree with you.   **(3 marks)**

....

....

....

....

....

....

....

....

Muslim attitudes to fertility treatments

1   Do you think all religious people should agree with infertility treatment?
Give **two** reasons for your point of view.   **(b, 4 marks)**

....

....

....

....

....

....

....

> Remember that you can use Muslims as your example in this question.

EXAM ALERT

2   Choose one religion other than Christianity and explain why some of its followers disagree with infertility treatment and some do not.   **(c, 8 marks)**

> Students have struggled with exam questions similar to this - be prepared! **ResultsPlus**

....

....

....

....

....

....

....

....

....

....

....

....

....

....

....

> You will also be marked on how well organised your answer is, on how clearly you use language and on your spelling, punctuation and grammar so make sure you give yourself time to check these.

Transplant surgery

1   What is **organ donation**?   (a, 2 marks)

....

....

> **Guided**

2   Do you think that organ donation should be encouraged?
Give **two** reasons for your point of view.   (b, 4 marks)

I .... that organ donation should be encouraged because ....

....

For example ....

I also think that ....

....

....

3   'All religious people should donate their organs when they die.' In your answer you should
refer to at least one religion.

   (i)   Do you agree? Give reasons for your opinion.   (d, 3 marks)

....

....

....

....

....

....

....

....

> Don't forget to show
> awareness in your answer of
> how controversial an issue
> organ donation is, and make
> sure that the two parts of your
> answer really do give different
> opinions.

   (ii)   Give reasons why some people may disagree with you.   (3 marks)

....

....

....

....

....

....

Christian attitudes to transplant surgery

> **Guided** 1   Explain why some Christians support organ donation and some do not.   **(c, 8 marks)**

Christians are divided on whether organ donation is
acceptable. Some argue it is acceptable because

....

....

They use evidence such as ....

....

....

Another reason is ....

....

....

....

Others believe it is wrong because ....

....

They will point to reasons such as ....

....

....

They might also believe that...

....

....

....

> Read the question carefully.
> This (c) style question asks you
> to give both sides of a debate.

> Try to clearly explain the
> reasons why Christians agree
> and disagree with organ
> donation. Use phrases such
> as 'because.' To support your
> points you could refer to the
> Bible, God and the teachings
> of Jesus in your answer.

Muslim attitudes to transplant surgery

> **Guided** 1 'Religious believers should always support organ donation.' In your answer you should refer to at least one religion.

(i) Do you agree? Give reasons for your point of view.   **(d, 3 marks)**

I agree because I think everyone including religious believers should support organ

donation because ....

....

A second reason for my opinion is ....

....

....

Also, ...

....

....

(ii) Give reasons why some people may disagree with you.   **(3 marks)**

One reason why people may disagree with my opinion is ....

....

....

A second reason to support this view is ....

....

....

Finally ....

....

....

Key words

Look carefully at the key words and their definitions below – can you connect the correct key word on the left with its corresponding definition on the right?

Word   **Definition**

Word	Definition
1) artificial insemination	a) the act of creating the universe or the universe which has been created
2) conservation	b) the increase in the temperature of the Earth's atmosphere (thought to be caused by the greenhouse effect)
3) creation	c) giving organs to be used in transplant surgery
4) embryo	d) not being able to have children
5) environment	e) protecting and preserving natural resources and the environment
6) global warming	f) an arrangement whereby a woman bears a child on behalf of another woman OR where an egg is donated and fertilised by the husband through IVF and then implanted into the wife's uterus
7) infertility	g) naturally occurring materials, such as oil and fertile land, which can be used by humans
8) in-vitro fertilisation (IVF)	h) looking after something so it can be passed on to the next generation
9) natural resources	i) a fertilised egg in the first eight weeks after conception
10) organ donation	j) the surroundings in which plants and animals live and on which they depend to live
11) stewardship	k) the method of fertilising a human egg in a test tube
12) surrogacy	l) injecting semen into the uterus by artificial means

Why do wars occur?

1 What is meant by **aggression**? **(a, 2 marks)**

....

....

....

2 What is meant by **exploitation**? **(a, 2 marks)**

....

....

....

....

> These terms are often seen to be reasons for the cause of war in the world today so think about what they mean in relation to this.

3 Do you think wars are ever necessary?
Give **two** reasons for your point of view. **(b, 4 marks)**

....

....

....

....

> Think carefully about the reasons why nations go to war when answering this question and remember to give your own opinion.

....

....

....

....

The United Nations (UN) and world peace

1   What is meant by **conflict resolution**?   **(a, 2 marks)**

....

....

....

> Remember that these two terms are the main aims of the peacekeeping organisation: the United Nations.

2   What is meant by **reconciliation**?   **(a, 2 marks)**

....

....

....

3   Do you think the UN has helped world peace?
    Give **two** reasons for your point of view.   **(b, 4 marks)**

....

....

....

....

....

....

....

> You could give examples in your answer to back up the reasons you give for your opinion.

Religious organisations and world peace

Guided **1** Explain how religious organisations work to promote world peace. **(c, 8 marks)**

Many religious organisations promote world peace by

....

....

....

....

> To answer this question use specific examples of religious organisations and explain how they promote world peace and what they have done. Try to mention up to four things that religious organisations have done.

One Christian organisation that promotes world peace is

....

One way they have promoted world peace is through discussion where ....

....

....

The have tried to put Christian teachings into action by ....

....

....

Another religious organisation that has worked for world peace is ....

....

They have tried to promote world peace through opposing war and violence. They do this by

....

because ....

....

....

2 Do you think there will ever be world peace?
Give **two** reasons for your point of view. **(b, 4 marks)**

....

....

....

....

....

Just war theory

1   Do you think all wars are just?
    Give **two** reasons for your point of view.   **(b, 4 marks)**

    ....

    ....

    ....

    ....

    ....

    ....

> Start your answer by stating what your opinion is.

> **Guided**

2   'There can never be a just war.' In your answer you should refer to at least one religion.

    (i) Do you agree?
             Give reasons for your opinion.   **(d, 3 marks)**

    I agree as I do not believe there is ever a good enough reason to go to war. I believe

    ....

    ....

    Secondly, even if you stick to the just war theory rules, people always get hurt. I think
    this because ....

    ....

    Finally, ...

    ....

    (ii) Give reasons why some people may disagree with you.   **(3 marks)**

    However, many Muslims feel some wars have to be
    fought and are therefore just. They believe ....

    ....

    ....

> Make sure you show awareness of what criteria has to be met in order for it to be considered a just war.

    Many Christians will argue that some wars are just if everything else has been tried first.
    War would be a ....

    ....

    ....

    Some Christians may also agree with just war theory because ....

    ....

    ....

Christian attitudes to war

1   What is meant by **weapons of mass destruction**?   **(a, 2 marks)**

....

....

....

> **Guided**

2   Do you think Christians should ever fight in wars?
    Give **two** reasons for your point of view.   **(b, 4 marks)**

I believe that Christians should not fight in wars if they are

following their religion fully. The Bible says ....

....

which teaches that ....

| Think about Christian teachings about war and make sure you give two **different** reasons for your opinion. |

....

A second reason why I believe Christians should not fight in wars is because..........................

....

....

....

Muslim attitudes to war

> **Guided**   1   'A religious person should not fight in a war.' In your answer you should refer to one religion other than Christianity.

(i)   Do you agree? Give reasons for your opinion.   (d, 3 marks)

I .... with the statement. I think that ....

....

....

....

....

....

....

....

....

> Read the question carefully! Here you are asked to refer to one religion **other than** Christianity. Lots of students miss this and so don't answer the question successfully.

(ii) Give reasons why some people may disagree with you.   (3 marks)

On the other hand ....

....

....

....

....

....

....

....

82

Christian attitudes to bullying

1   What is **bullying**?   (a, 2 marks)

....

....

....

....

> Remember to learn your key words thoroughly to answer (a) questions and also to help you explain key ideas.

> **Guided**

2   Explain why Christians are always against bullying.   (c, 8 marks)

Christians believe that bullying is always wrong because it goes against Christian teachings such as ....

....

....

....

Also Christians believe that ....

....

....

....

The example and teachings of Jesus say that ....

....

....

....

A final reason why bullying is seen by Christians as wrong is because ....

....

....

....

> Make sure you refer to Christian teachings about why bullying is always wrong. Don't just list ideas, make sure you explain them by using phrases such as 'because' and perhaps use examples to back up your reasons.

Had a go ☐   Nearly there ☐   Nailed it! ☐

Muslim attitudes to bullying

1 What is meant by **respect**?   **(a, 2 marks)**

....

....

....

 2 Do you think we should do more to help the victims of bullying?
Give **two** reasons for your point of view.   **(b, 4 marks)**

I think that ....

This is because ....

....

Also, ...

> Remember to offer a short but
> accurate explanation of the
> term given.

....

....

....

Religious conflict within families

1   Do you think religion is the biggest source of family conflict?
    Give **two** reasons for your point of view.   **(b, 4 marks)**

....

....

....

....

....

....

2   Explain why religion causes conflict in families.   **(c, 8 marks)**

....

....

....

....

....

....

....

Remember that this is an 'explain' question so requires your answer to be detailed and thorough. Start a new paragraph for each new point you make. This will make it easier to check that what you have said is really clear and answers the question.

....

....

....

....

....

....

....

....

....

Read back through your answer. Have you used key words to help your explanation? Is your answer clear and well-organised?

Had a go ☐   Nearly there ☐   Nailed it! ☐

Christian teachings on forgiveness and reconciliation

1   Explain why forgiveness and reconciliation are so important to Christians.   **(c, 8 marks)**

....

....

....

....

> This type of question is worth the highest number of marks so make sure you read it carefully, plan out your answer and spend sufficient time answering it.

....

....

....

....

....

....

....

....

....

....

....

....

Muslim teachings on forgiveness and reconciliation

1   Do you think some things are unforgiveable?
    Give **two** reasons for your point of view.   **(b, 4 marks)**

    ....

    ....

    ....

    ....

    ....

    ....

Guided   2   'Religious believers should always forgive those who do wrong against them.' In your
    answer you should refer to one religion other than Christianity.

    (i) Do you agree? Give reasons for your opinion.   **(d, 3 marks)**

    I disagree with the statement because I think there are some actions that are

    unforgiveable such as ....

    because ....

    ....   ,,,,,,,,,,..

    I also think that some people do not deserve forgiveness because ....,,,,,,,,   .,,,

    ....

    Religious believers are human and have feelings and it may be very hard to move on from

    some events therefore ....

    ....

    (ii) Give reasons why some people may disagree with you.   **(3 marks)**

    On the other hand, some Muslims may disagree with me. Forgiveness is a key religious

    teaching in most world religions including Islam. They teach ....

    ....

    Another teaching in Islam about forgiveness is .... ,,,,,,,,..

    ....

    ....

    Also ....

    ....

    ....

Key words

Look carefully at the key words and their definitions below – can you connect the correct key word on the left with its corresponding definition on the right?

Word

Definition

| 1) aggression |
| 2) bullying |
| 3) conflict resolution |
| 4) exploitation |
| 5) forgiveness |
| 6) just war |
| 7) pacifism |
| 8) reconciliation |
| 9) respect |
| 10) the United Nations |
| 11) weapons of mass destruction |
| 12) world peace |

a) stopping blaming someone and/or pardoning them for what they have done wrong

b) bringing together people who were opposed to each other

c) the ending of war throughout the whole world (the basic aim of the United Nations)

d) the belief that all disputes should be settled by peaceful means

e) taking advantage of a weaker group

f) bringing a fight or struggle to a peaceful conclusion

g) intimidating/frightening people weaker than yourself

h) weapons which can destroy large areas and numbers of people

i) a war which is fought for the right reasons and in a right way

j) an international body set up to promote world peace and cooperation

k) attacking without being provoked

l) treating a person or their feelings with consideration

The need for law and justice

1 What is meant by **responsibility**?   (a, 2 marks)

....

....

....

....

> Remember to learn your key words thoroughly to do well on these (a) questions but also to help you explain points in your other questions.

2 What is **justice**?   (a, 2 marks)

....

....

....

3 Explain why justice is important in society.   (c, 8 marks)

....

....

....

....

> These (c) type questions are worth the most marks so make sure you spend enough time answering them.

....

....

....

....

....

....

....

....

....

....

....

Theories of punishment

1   What is **retribution**?   **(a, 2 marks)**

....

....

....

 2   Do you think all criminals need to go to prison?
Give **two** reasons for your point of view.   **(b, 4 marks)**

I agree/disagree* because ....

....

....

A second reason why I think this is because ....

....

....

....

> Make sure you develop the reasons you offer in your answer by giving relevant examples or extra information to explain your view.

> * Delete the option that doesn't apply to you.

3   Do you think criminals should be given the chance to reform?
Give **two** reasons for your point of view.   **(b, 4 marks)**

....

....

....

....

....

....

Christians and justice

1 What is **judgement**?   **(a, 2 marks)**

....

....

....

Guided

2 Explain the importance of justice to Christians.   **(c, 8 marks)**

Justice is important to Christians. This is shown in the teachings of the Bible which say ....

....

....

....

Jesus also taught that ....

....

....

....

Christians also believe that God ....

....

....

....

Many Christians choose to put their beliefs into practice for justice showing how important

it is by ....

....

....

> You could start a new paragraph for each point you make. This will make it easier to go back and read through your answer to make sure it is clear and that you've said what you wanted.

91

Muslims and justice

1   Do you think religious people should do more to prevent injustice in the world?
Give **two** reasons for your point of view.   **(b, 4 marks)**

....

....

....

....

....

....

> Make clear that this is your own opinion, for example 'I think that…' or 'In my opinion…'

2   'Religious believers should always fight for justice and equality.'
In your answer you should refer to one religion other than Christianity.

(i)   Do you agree? Give reasons for your opinion.   **(d, 3 marks)**

....

....

....

....

....

....

....

....

> Make sure you read the question carefully. This (d) style question asks you to refer to one religion **other** than Christianity.

(ii) Give reasons why some people may disagree with you.   **(3 marks)**

....

....

....

....

....

....

....

....

> The best answers give up to three reasons for their opinion and for why people disagree, as well as giving enough detail to explain each point clearly.

Non-religious arguments about capital punishment

1   What is **capital punishment**?   (a, 2 marks)

....

....

....

2   Do you agree with capital punishment for society's most severe crimes?
    Give **two** reasons for your point of view.   (b, 4 marks)

....   ┌─────────────────────────┐
                                                                                            │ You should give two well │
....   │ thought out reasons to   │
                                                                                            │ support your view.   │
....   └─────────────────────────┘

....

....

....

....

3   Do you think capital punishment should be legal in the UK?
    Give **two** reasons for your point of view.   (b, 4 marks)

....

....

....

....

....

....

Christian attitudes to capital punishment

1 'Religious believers should always oppose capital punishment.' In your answer you should refer to at least one religion.

> Students have struggled with exam questions similar to this - be prepared! **ResultsPlus**

(i) Do you agree? Give reasons for your opinion.   **(d, 3 marks)**

I think that religious believers should disagree with capital punishment because ....

....

....

Christians may also refer to the sanctity of life argument suggesting ....

....

....

Finally, one of the main teachings of Christianity is about love and forgiveness, therefore

....

....

(ii) Give reasons why some people may disagree with you.   **(3 marks)**

However some people disagree with my views and suggest that capital punishment is a good thing because ....

....

Some Christians may support capital punishment because of the teachings in the Bible which state ....

....

Some Christians may also suggest that capital punishment is acceptable in circumstances such as ....

....

Muslim attitudes to capital punishment

Guided 1 Choose one religion other than Christianity and explain why some of its followers support capital punishment and some do not. **(c, 8 marks)**

Muslims are divided over the issue of capital punishment. Some Muslims support capital punishment because the Qur'an teaches ....

....

....

....

> This question asks you to explain why some religious believers **do** support capital punishment and why some **do not**. You could give examples from both sides to offer a full explanation.

A second reason why some Muslims would support capital punishment is because ....

....

....

....

Muslims may also think that ....

....

....

....

Other Muslims may oppose capital punishment because ....

....

....

....

Drugs and alcohol laws

1   Do you think that people under 18 should be allowed to drink alcohol?
    Give **two** reasons to support your point of view.   **(b, 4 marks)**

    ....

    ....

    ....

    ....

    ....

    ....

    ....

2   'Drugs should be banned because they lead to social and health problems.'
    In your answer you should refer to at least one religion.

    (i) Do you agree? Give reasons for your opinion.   **(d, 3 marks)**

    ....

    ....

    ....

    ....

    ....

    ....

    ....

    ....

    (ii) Give reasons why some people may disagree with you.   **(3 marks)**

    ....

    ....

    ....

    ....

    ....

    ....

    ....

Social and health problems caused by drugs and alcohol

1   Explain why drugs cause social and health problems.   **(c, 8 marks)**

....

....

....

....

....

....

....

....

....

....

....

....

....

....

....

Christian attitudes to drugs and alcohol

Guided 1 Explain why some Christians choose not to drink alcohol. **(c, 8 marks)**

Many Christians choose not to drink because they believe the Bible teaches ....

....

....

....

> Try to build your answer up, giving as many reasons as you can. Make sure you actually explain each reason rather than just describing them.

Some Christians believe alcohol damages the human body by ....

....

....

....

They may choose not to drink alcohol because ....

....

....

....

A further reason why ....

....

....

....

Muslim attitudes to drugs and alcohol

> **Guided**

1 Do you think that drinking alcohol damages health?
Give **two** reasons for your point of view.   **(b, 4 marks)**

I think that drinking alcohol ....

This is because ....

....

....

I also think that ....

....

....

2 Do you think religious people should drink alcohol?
Give **two** reasons for your point of view.   **(b, 4 marks)**

....

....

....

....

....

....

....

Think about the religious
beliefs you've studied in class
and use these to support
your opinion. You could try
to answer this by referring to
Muslims.

Had a go ☐ **Nearly there** ☐ **Nailed it!** ☐

Key words

Look carefully at the key words and their definitions below – can you connect the correct key word on the left with its corresponding definition on the right?

Word

Definition

1) addiction	a) the death penalty for a crime or offence
2) capital punishment	b) restore to normal life
3) crime	c) due allocation of reward and punishment / the maintenance of what is right
4) deterrence	d) the idea that punishments should make criminals pay for what they have done wrong
5) judgement	e) the idea that punishments should try to change criminals so that they will not commit crimes again
6) justice	f) an act against the law
7) law	g) an act against the will of God
8) reform	h) the act of judging people and their actions
9) rehabilitation	i) being responsible for one's actions
10) responsibility	j) rules made by Parliament and enforceable by the courts
11) retribution	k) a recurring compulsion to engage in an activity regardless of its bad effects
12) sin	l) the idea that punishments should be of such a nature that they will put people off (deter) committing crimes

Exam skills: (a) questions and SPaG

Guided   1   What is **forgiveness**?   (a, 2 marks)

> Forgiveness is when you say sorry to someone.

> These (a) type questions require a short but accurate definition of a given term. This is why it is important to learn your key words thoroughly. This student answer does not give a full explanation of the term.

> Can you improve it in the space below?

Forgiveness is ....

....

....

....

Spelling, punctuation and grammar

> Try to answer the question below, thinking particularly about your **spelling**, **punctuation** and **grammar.**

Guided   2   Do you think the Ten Commandments are still relevant to life today?
Give **two** reasons for your point of view.   (b, 4 marks)

I think the Ten Commandments are .... relevant to life today. This is because

....

....

....

A second reason for my opinion is that ....

....

....

....

> In Section 1 of the Unit 8 exam paper, there are 4 marks available for spelling, punctuation and grammar. To be successful here, your spelling, punctuation and grammar need to be really good. You need to use these to help make what you want to say very clear. Try to also use a good range of key words accurately.

Exam skills: (b) questions

⟩ **Guided** ⟩ 1 Do you think it is always possible to forgive?
Give **two** reasons for your point of view.

(b, 4 marks)

> I think that forgiveness is difficult in some situations as some actions are too horrible to forgive.

This response is very brief and not developed at all. The student has given a very simple reason for their opinion but needs to develop it by explaining perhaps a circumstance where forgiveness is not possible because the action is so awful (e.g. murder). Also, in order to achieve success in this answer and the full marks available, a second reason for the student's opinion is required.

See if you can improve the answer in the space below.

....

....

....

....

....

....

....

Have you:

• Offered an **opinion**?

• Offered **two** different reasons for the opinion?

• **Developed** each reason by explaining it?

• Used an example to support each reason?

Exam skills: (c) questions

Guided   1   Explain why some Christians agree with genetic engineering and some do not.

(c, 8 marks)

> Some Christians would agree with genetic engineering as it could save lives. This is important as life is special as it was made by God. Also, as long as it doesn't hurt someone, then they would support it.
>
> Other Christians may disagree as they do not think humans have the right to mess around with life.

The answer begins well and the student shows some understanding of why some Christians agree and others disagree. However, the reasons offered are too brief and are not developed, for example the second part of the answer seems to simply describe rather than explain a reason why Christians might not support genetic engineering. This question is worth 8 marks so you need to spend time answering it and can make up to four points.

See if you can improve the answer in the space below.

....

....

....

....

....

....

....

....

....

....

....

....

....

....

Remember that in every (c) question in the Unit 8 paper, you will also be assessed on the quality of your written communication (QWC). This means that you need to make sure that what you want to say is well organised and very clear. Try to also use any key words accurately. Go back over your finished answer and check that you're happy with all these points.

Exam skills: (d) questions

> **Guided** 1 'Religious people should not drive cars.' In your answer you should refer to at least one religion.

(i) Do you agree? Give reasons for your opinion. **(d, 3 marks)**

> I disagree as I believe cars are necessary in life today and religious believers are included in this. They may need their cars to get to work and they should not be afraid to do this because of the damage it causes to the environment. Today, there are more environmentally friendly fuels which lessen the impact on the environment or they could use an electric car which would not damage the environment.

(ii) Give reasons why some people may disagree with you. **(3 marks)**

> On the other hand, it is because of things like cars that our planet is getting damaged by pollution and Christians believe in stewardship which is to care for the environment. Perhaps they should consider what impact they have on the world by driving cars.

> Overall, this is a good attempt. In the first part the student gives their opinion and two different reasons for it, one of which is developed. The second part focuses on the question but is not detailed. To improve this answer, the student would need to develop the second reason in the first part or add another reason and also expand section two.

> Now write your own answer in the space below first of all agreeing with the statement.

(i) ....

....

....

....

....

....

....

(ii) ....

....

....

....

....

....

UNIT 1
Practice exam paper

Edexcel publishes official Sample Assessment Material on its website. This practice exam paper has been written to help you practise what you have learned and may not be representative of a real exam paper.

> **Time:** 1 hour 30 minutes
> Answer **ONE** question from each of the four sections

> Try to spend about 20 minutes answering each section. Where you see *, you will be assessed on your quality of written communication.

Section 1 Believing in God

You will be assessed on your spelling, punctuation and grammar in this section

EITHER

1 (a) What does **omni-benevolent** mean?   (2 marks)

   (b) Do you think a religious upbringing makes children believe in God?
        Give **two** reasons for your point of view.   (4 marks)

  *(c) Explain how miracles may lead to belief in God.   (8 marks)

   (d) 'Evil and suffering prove that God does not exist.'
        In your answer you should refer to at least one religion.

        (i) Do you agree? Give reasons for your opinion.   (3 marks)

        (ii) Give reasons why some people may disagree with you.   (3 marks)

        Spelling, punctuation and grammar   (4 marks)

OR

2 (a) What is meant by the term **miracle**?   (2 marks)

   (b) Do you think the media should be allowed to show religion in a
        negative way? Give **two** reasons for your point of view.   (4 marks)

  *(c) Explain how unanswered prayers may cause a problem for belief in God.   (8 marks)

   (d) 'The universe must have been created by God.' In your answer you
        should refer to Christianity.

        (i) Do you agree? Give reasons for your opinion.   (3 marks)

        (ii) Give reasons why some people may disagree with you.   (3 marks)

        Spelling, punctuation and grammar.   (4 marks)

                                                             (Total for Section 1 = 24 marks)

Section 2 Matters of life and death

EITHER

3 (a) What is meant by **quality of life**?   (2 marks)

   (b) Do you agree with abortion? Give **two** reasons for your point of view.   (4 marks)

  *(c) Explain why followers of **one** *religion other than Christianity* believe
        in life after death.   (8 marks)

   (d) 'The media should not be allowed to criticise what religions say about
        matters of life and death.' In your answer you should refer to at least
        one religion.

   (i) Do you agree? Give reasons for your opinion. (3 marks)

   (ii) Give reasons why some people may disagree with you. (3 marks)

OR

4 **(a)** What is **reincarnation**? (2 marks)

   (b) Do you think everyone should believe in the afterlife? Give **two** reasons
   for your point of view. (4 marks)

   *(c)** Explain why some Christians do not agree with abortion. (8 marks)

   (d) 'The law on euthanasia should be changed.' In your answer you should
   refer to at least one religion.

   (i) Do you agree? Give reasons for your opinion. (3 marks)

   (ii) Give reasons why some people may disagree with you. (3 marks)

   (Total for Section 2 = 20 marks)

Section 3 Marriage and the family

EITHER

5 **(a)** What is **adultery**? (2 marks)

   (b) Do you think divorce is better than an unhappy marriage? Give **two** reasons
   for your point of view. (4 marks)

   *(c)** Choose **one** *religion other than Christianity* and explain why some of its
   followers accept the use of contraception and some do not. (8 marks)

   (d) 'Everyone should accept homosexuality in society today.' In your answer
   you should refer to at least one religion.

   (i) Do you agree? Give reasons for your opinion. (3 marks)

   (ii) Give reasons why some people may disagree with you. (3 marks)

OR

6 **(a)** What is meant by **pre-marital sex**? (2 marks)

   (b) Do you think marriage is still important in the UK today?
   Give **two** reasons for your point of view. (4 marks)

   *(c)** Explain why some Christians allow divorce and others do not. (8 marks)

   (d) 'Family life is important for making sure children are brought up correctly.'
   In your answer you should refer to at least one religion.

   (i) Do you agree? Give reasons for your opinion. (3 marks)

   (ii) Give reasons why some people may disagree with you. (3 marks)

   (Total for Section 3 = 20 marks)

Section 4 Religion and community cohesion

EITHER

7 **(a)** What is meant by **racial harmony**? (2 marks)

   (b) Do you think living in a multi-faith society causes problems for religious
   people? Give **two** reasons for your point of view. (4 marks)

   *(c)** Explain why the government works to promote community cohesion. (8 marks)

   (d) 'If everyone were religious, there would be no racism.' In your answer
   you should refer to at least one religion.

   (i) Do you agree? Give reasons for your opinion. (3 marks)

(ii) Give reasons why some people may disagree with you. (3 marks)

OR

8 (a) What is meant by **discrimination**? (2 marks)

(b) Do you think the government should do more to promote community cohesion in the UK? Give **two** reasons for your point of view. (4 marks)

*(c) Choose **one** *religion other than Christianity* and explain why the followers of that religion should promote racial harmony. (8 marks)

(d) 'Men and women will never be equal in the UK.' In your answer you should refer to at least one religion.

(i) Do you agree? Give reasons for your opinion. (3 marks)

(ii) Give reasons why some people may disagree with you. (3 marks)

(Total for Section 4 = 20 marks)

UNIT 8
Practice exam paper

Edexcel publishes official Sample Assessment Material on its website. This practice exam paper has been written to help you practise what you have learned and may not be representative of a real exam paper.

Time: 1 hour 30 minutes
Answer **ONE** question from each of the four sections

Try to spend about 20 minutes answering each section. Where you see *, you will be assessed on your quality of written communication.

Section 1 Rights and responsibilities

You will be assessed on your spelling, punctuation and grammar in this section

EITHER

1 (a) What are **human rights**?   (2 marks)

   (b) Do you think it is important to vote in elections?
        Give **two** reasons for your point of view.   (4 marks)

   *(c) Explain how Christians make moral decisions.   (8 marks)

   (d) 'Christians should never support cloning.'
        In your answer you should refer to at least one religion.

        (i) Do you agree? Give reasons for your opinion.   (3 marks)

        (ii) Give reasons why some people may disagree with you.   (3 marks)

        Spelling, punctuation and grammar.   (4 marks)

OR

2 (a) What is a **pressure group**?   (2 marks)

   (b) Do you think Christians should do more to help show the importance of
        human rights? Give **two** reasons for your point of view.   (4 marks)

   *(c) Choose **one** religion and explain why some of its followers will use Situation Ethics
         to make moral decisions and some will not.   (8 marks)

   (d) 'The Bible is not relevant today.' In your answer you should refer to Christianity.

        (i) Do you agree? Give reasons for your opinion.   (3 marks)

        (ii) Give reasons why some people may disagree with you.   (3 marks)

        Spelling, punctuation and grammar.   (4 marks)

                                                    (Total for Section 1 = 24 marks)

Section 2 Environmental and medical issues

EITHER

3 (a) What is **surrogacy**?   (2 marks)

   (b) Do you think pollution is the biggest environmental problem facing the
        planet today? Give **two** reasons for your point of view.   (4 marks)

   *(c) Choose **one** religion and explain why its followers believe it is important to care for
         the environment.   (8 marks)

(d) 'Everyone should be willing to donate their organs after death.' In your answer you should refer to at least one religion.

    (i) Do you agree? Give reasons for your opinion.   (3 marks)

    (ii) Give reasons why some people may disagree with you.   (3 marks)

OR

4 (a) What is **global warming**?   (2 marks)

  (b) Do you think everyone has a responsibility to care for the environment? Give **two** reasons for your point of view.   (4 marks)

  *(c) Explain why some Christians may seek medical treatment for infertility and some will not.   (8 marks)

  (d) 'One person alone cannot help the environment, so there is no point trying.' In your answer you should refer to at least one religion.

    (i) Do you agree? Give reasons for your opinion.   (3 marks)

    (ii) Give reasons why some people may disagree with you.   (3 marks)

         (Total for Section 2 = 20 marks)

Section 3 Peace and conflict

EITHER

5 (a) What is **pacifism**?   (2 marks)

  (b) Do you think there will ever be world peace? Give **two** reasons for your point of view.   (4 marks)

  *(c) Choose **one** *religion other than Christianity* and explain why its followers are against bullying.   (8 marks)

  (d) 'The United Nations has done more to encourage peace than religion has.' In your answer you should refer to at least one religion.

    (i) Do you agree? Give reasons for your opinion.   (3 marks)

    (ii) Give reasons why some people may disagree with you.   (3 marks)

OR

6 (a) What is **world peace**?   (2 marks)

  (b) Do you think forgiveness is important? Give **two** reasons for your point of view.   (4 marks)

  *(c) Choose **one** *religion other than Christianity* and explain why some of its followers will not fight in a war.   (8 marks)

  (d) 'Bullies deserve sympathy not punishment.' In your answer you should refer to at least one religion.

    (i) Do you agree? Give reasons for your opinion.   (3 marks)

    (ii) Give reasons why some people may disagree with you.   (3 marks)

         (Total for Section 3 = 20 marks)

Section 4 Crime and punishment

EITHER

7 (a) What is meant by **rehabilitation**?   (2 marks)

  (b) Do you think punishment changes people's behaviour? Give **two** reasons for your point of view.   (4 marks)

  *(c) Choose **one** *religion other than Christianity* and explain why justice is important to its followers.   (8 marks)

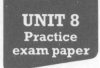

(d) 'Not all criminals should go to prison.' In your answer you should refer to at least one religion.

    (i) Do you agree? Give reasons for your opinion.   (3 marks)

    (ii) Give reasons why some people may disagree with you.   (3 marks)

OR

8 **(a)** What is meant by **reform**?   (2 marks)

  (b) Do you think capital punishment should be allowed in the UK? Give **two** reasons for your point of view.   (4 marks)

  (c) Explain why some Christians drink alcohol and some do not.   (8 marks)

  (d) 'The law needs to be tougher on criminals.' In your answer you should refer to at least one religion.

    (i) Do you agree? Give reasons for your opinion.   (3 marks)

    (ii) Give reasons why some people may disagree with you.   (3 marks)

(Total for Section 4 = 20 marks)

Answers

Here we have given examples of possible responses, however other approaches may also be suitable. The number given to each topic refers to its page number.

UNIT 1
Believing in God

1. Introduction
1   Agnosticism is when a person is not sure whether God exists or not and therefore whether to believe in God.
2   Omni-benevolent is a term used to describe God meaning he is all-good or all-loving.
3   *Agree*:
   - Everyone should believe in God as it gives hope and comfort.
   - Belief in God can lead to belief in other things such as rules and guidance.
   - Belief in God and therefore religion will allow a person to go to Heaven after death.

   Disagree:
   - People should be allowed to believe what they want.
   - Belief in God may be worthless as we do not know whether he is real.
   - There are many negative aspects to religion so people should not believe in God.

2. Religious upbringing
1   *Agree*:
   - Christian parents will want their children to be Christians and believe in God because it is the only way to get to Heaven.
   - It allows the faith to continue and be passed on from one generation to another.

   Disagree:
   - Children should be allowed to make their own choices about their faith.
   - Faith should not be forced on anyone – they should choose it freely.
   - Children may rebel against religion and their family if it is forced on them.
2   *Agree*:
   - A religious upbringing teaches children how to behave and act towards others.
   - Religion provides structure and guidance.
   - Christians believe God intends them to marry, have children and raise them within the Christian faith.

   Disagree:
   - There are many other ways of finding out about God e.g. the Bible, attending church.
   - It may be difficult for children to always please their parents and they may rebel.
   - There is no evidence to suggest a religious upbringing is best.

3. Religious experiences
1   This is something a person undergoes where they believe they have some connection with God that convinces them he is real – for example, a miracle.
2   Conversion is when a person's life is changed in some way by an experience of God.
3   - It is a form of communication with God.
   - An experience may strengthen a person's faith or even convert people to faith.
   - Different types of experiences allow people to get to know God in different ways.
   - Many experiences may convince a person that God is real as he is the only explanation for an event.
   - Examples that may be included: prayer, miracles, numinous experiences, conversion.

4. The design argument
1   *Agree*:
   - Science explains that humans and everything in the world evolved and therefore God is not needed to explain how the universe got here.
   - Design in the world could be due to chance rather than actual planning.

   Disagree:
   - Science is still a theory that is as unproven as God's existence.
   - There is too much evidence of design in the world for it to have happened by chance (e.g. Paley's watch).
   - The Big Bang is still just a theory, rather than proven fact.
2   *Agree*:
   - The world is too perfect to have happened by chance as science explains.
   - Sources such as the Bible suggest that God is the only explanation needed.

   Disagree:
   - Other explanations offered by science may be just as possible to accept.
   - If God designed the world why are there design flaws like earthquakes?

5. The causation argument
1   *Agree*:
   - God explains everything in the universe and the specialness of humans.
   - Even science does not explain everything about the world.

   Disagree:
   - Other explanations offered by science are just as credible as God.

- We cannot prove that God is real which makes it difficult to accept he created the universe.

2 *Agree*:
- God offers a full explanation as to how and why the world came to exist.
- God planning and designing the universe makes sense with all the evidence of design in the world.
- Everything in the world is seen to have a cause and reason for existing so God makes sense.

Disagree:
- If God created the universe, there is an unanswered question of 'what caused God?'
- Science offers us an alternative explanation for the universe.
- We cannot prove God is real which means he may not have caused the universe.

6. The origins of the world

1 • Other Christians believe the only way to respond to scientific criticisms of the origin of the world is to reject science and argue the Bible tells them the truth.
- Science and religion can be compatible as the Big Bang caused the world but God caused the Big Bang.
- They may argue that scientific theories of creation were part of God's plan for the creation of the universe.
- Some Christians believe the Genesis story of creation is not literally true and is more storylike.
- They accept that science tells us how the world came to exist and religion why.

7. Unanswered prayers

1 *Yes*:
- It can bring hope and comfort in times of need.
- Religious believers pray regularly to develop a relationship with God.

No:
- We do not know if God is even real.
- Many prayers are not answered meaning it is pointless.

2 • Atheists would argue that unanswered prayers are evidence God does not exist. If he cared for humans he would help.
- Many may question their faith and conclude that God cannot exist.
- Many people experience pain and suffering in their lives and question where God is in these times.
- The sheer amount of suffering in the world convinces them that God cannot be real.

8. The problem of evil and suffering

1 Natural evil is evil acts that are not caused by humans but which cause suffering.

2 *Yes*:
- If God cared for humans he would not allow them to suffer so excessively.
- It is very hard to accept natural evil which is not human responsibility.

No:
- Perhaps evil and suffering are God's plan, which humans are not aware of.
- Perhaps God cannot intervene in the world because humans have freewill.

9. Christian responses to the problem of evil and suffering

1 Free will is the idea that humans are free to make their own choices and decisions and things are not set in place by God.

2 *Christianity*:
- They may accept that God has a plan they are not aware of.
- They may argue that God gave humans free will and sometimes evil and suffering results.
- They may try to follow the example set by Jesus and help others.
- They may try to strengthen their faith.
- They may pray and worship more regularly.

10. The media and belief in God

1 *Yes*:
- TV may be biased, either for or against religion and God.
- For many, TV is how they learn about ideas such as God.

No:
- People can think for themselves and know what is true and what is not.
- Other things influence people more.

2 *Agree*:
- It often portrays religious believers as terrorists and extremists, for example, Panorama and Scientology.
- The media doesn't always show the truth as they can be biased.
- Religion is often made fun of or ridiculed.
- People in the media don't always understand religion correctly.

Disagree:
- Most religions are portrayed accurately.
- Advice is often sought when portraying religion or religious issues.
- There are many TV programmes that show positive aspects of religion, for example, the BBC's 'The Bible's Buried Secrets'.

11. Key words

1, d; 2, i; 3, b; 4, a; 5, l; 6, c; 7, e; 8, k; 9, h; 10, g; 11, f; 12, j.

Matters of life and death

12. Christian beliefs in life after death
1 Resurrection is the belief that after death the body stays in the ground until the end of the world when it is raised.
2 *Agree*:
 - There is no evidence of life after death.
 - If this is the only life, we should make the most of it.
 - Many people accept science which suggests there is no afterlife.

 Disagree:
 - We have duties and responsibilities and cannot simply enjoy life.
 - The Bible gives us evidence of life after death.
 - We will be judged in the afterlife on how we have lived our lives.

13. The effect of belief in the afterlife on Christian lives
1
 - Christians believe they will be judged by God after death so try to live within the guidelines he has given in the Bible and guided by the Church.
 - They will try to treat others the way they would like to be treated and behave according to the laws of God through helping others.
 - The fact Jesus rose from the dead gives them hope that they can also achieve this and go to Heaven as a reward for the way they have lived their lives.
 - The possibility of an afterlife offers hope to Christians of being with their loved ones again so they can feel at peace with death.
 - The promise of Heaven offers an explanation for suffering experienced in life so they can feel at peace with their situation.

14. Islamic beliefs about life after death
1 *Yes*:
 - All religions teach of an afterlife.
 - It offer people something to aim for and work towards.
 - It means we can be at peace with death of loved ones.

 No:
 - Science shows that there is no evidence for life after death, so why should it be believed.
 - There is no definite proof of an afterlife as no-one has come back.
2 *Agree*:
 - This is what is taught by Christianity.
 - Islam teaches that the angel of death will take a person's soul to *barzakh* (the stage between when a person dies and when they face judgement).
 - Evidence from the paranormal e.g. ghosts.

Disagree:
 - Science tells us that humans are physical not spiritual.
 - There is no evidence of a soul.
 - Muslims believe both the body and soul survive.
 - Catholics also believe in resurrection.

15. Non-religious beliefs in life after death
1 A near death experience is when someone is about to die and has an out of body experience.
2
 - Paranormal experiences lead to belief in life after death.
 - Life after death is comforting.
 - It is seen as a reward for living a good life.
 - There must be something after this life.

16. Non-belief in life after death
1 *Yes*:
 - Evidence from religion and the Bible.
 - Evidence from Jesus' resurrection.
 No:
 - No physical or scientific evidence.
 - Those who believe in an afterlife like mediums are fake.
2 *Agree*:
 - No evidence.
 - We just live and then die.
 - Ghosts could be hallucinations.
 Disagree:
 - Mediums claim they can talk to dead people which is evidence of life after death.
 - If ghosts exists, dead people have some form after death.
 - Some people claim to remember ideas from past lives.
 - Both Muslims and Catholics believe that the body will be resurrected after death.

17. Abortion
1 *Yes*:
 - It is taking the life of another person which is wrong.
 - Life begins at conception.
 No:
 - Women have the right to choose what happens to their body.
 - It is sensible for the right reasons.
2 *Support*:
 - In cases of rape or incest.
 - Lesser of two evils.
 - In cases where the child may be disabled or the mothers health is at risk.
 - The woman has the right to choose what happens to her body.
 Oppose:
 - There are alternatives such as adoption.
 - Even disabled children can live happy lives.
 - An embryo should have rights.

- Life begins at conception and is sacred and therefore special.

18. Christian attitudes to abortion

1 This is the belief that life is holy and belongs to God.
2 *Agree*:
  - Religious people believe in the sanctity of life.
  - Abortion is taking a life which is against the Ten Commandments.
  - Christians are supposed to show love towards one another, including unborn babies.
  Disagree:
  - Not all religious people are against abortion.
  - Some would argue it is the lesser of two evils.
  - Abortion may be the most loving thing to do.

19. Muslim attitudes to abortion

1 *Islam*:
  - Sanctity of life – life is sacred and should be kept this way.
  - Ensoulment (120 days).
  - Abortion takes away life so is wrong.
  - An unplanned pregnancy is not an acceptable reason for an abortion.
  - All children have a right to be cared for.
  - Muslims are expected to have children.

20. Euthanasia

1 Voluntary euthanasia is when a person who has a terminal illness requests the right to end their life painlessly.
2 *Yes*:
  - It is murder and the taking of another life.
  - Life is always worth living.
  No:
  - Sometimes if it is their wish and they are in extreme pain, it is the kindest action.
  - Quality of life is important.

21. Christian attitudes to euthanasia

1 *Yes*:
  - Murder is against their teachings.
  - Only God has the right to take life.
  No:
  - Sometimes it is the kinder action.
  - Quality of life is important and in some cases if a person chooses euthanasia, it should be allowed.
2 *Agree*:
  - The law should be changed so people do the most loving thing (Situation Ethics).
  - There are some people who have not been prosecuted who have helped others commit euthanasia.
  - The law on euthanasia should become tougher so life support machines are not turned off.

Disagree:
  - Religious people view life as sacred and special (sanctity of life).
  - Only God should be allowed to take a person's life.
  - Doctors are trained to keep people alive.

22. Muslim attitudes to euthanasia

1 *Yes*:
  - Murder is against their teachings.
  - Only God has the right to take life.
  No:
  - Sometimes it is the kinder action.
  - Quality of life is important and in some cases if a person chooses euthanasia, it should be allowed.
2 *Islam*.
  Accept:
  - It may be kinder.
  - Some would argue that life support machines are sustaining a life that Allah has already taken.
  Don't accept:
  - Sanctity of life.
  - Suffering is a test.
  - Allah created life and only he can take it away.
  - They have a duty to care for the sick and elderly.

23. Matters of life and death in the media

1 *Yes*:
  - It is important to focus on and talk about these issues.
  - They are more prominent and important today.
  No:
  - There are too many views to show all of them.
  - Sometimes the wrong information might be given.
2 *Agree*:
  - Religious followers believe that what their religion teaches is right and to criticise this would cause offence. For example, Muslims believe in life after death because it is taught in the Qur'an – to criticise it would be very upsetting for Muslims.
  - Criticising religious beliefs in life and death could also offend Christians who may hold strong views about abortion and euthanasia. They may believe that these are against the Ten Commandments and against God's wishes.
  - The media should be allowed to present a range of religious ideas but not criticise them because this may give a biased view.
  Disagree:
  - It is wrong to present only one view on an issue because everyone should be entitled to form their own opinion and they can't do this if the information is one-sided.

- It is important to debate views on these issues as they are constantly changing and religious advice is not always helpful.
- Different religions believe different things, for example Christians believe in resurrection and others in reincarnation. People should be allowed to consider the alternatives.

24. Key words
1, i; 2, d; 3, l; 4, a; 5, k; 6, b; 7, g; 8, c; 9, h; 10, e; 11, j; 12, f.

Marriage and the family

25. Changing attitudes towards marriage, divorce, family and homosexuality in the UK
1 A nuclear family is a family that has a mother, father and children who live together.
2 A reconstituted family is where two sets of children become one family when their divorced parents marry each other. They become stepbrothers and stepsisters.
3 • More people are tolerant of different types of family today, rather than traditional family values.
- There are many new types of family today.
- There are more single parent families.
- Fathers are more involved in child care.
- Women have careers and may be the main wage earner.
- Some people do not live near their extended family.

26. Christian attitudes to sex outside marriage
1 *Yes*:
- Some people may want to show commitment but may not be ready for marriage.
- It is a way of expressing love for another person.
No:
- Sex is something special that should be saved for marriage.
- The purpose of sex is to have children who should be born within marriage.
2 *Agree*:
- Today's society is different and attitudes have changed towards marriage and sex
- Not many people today follow religious ideas making them out of date.
- It is unrealistic to wait until after marriage to have sex as couples choose to cohabit and show their love for each other.
Disagree:
- God intended sex to be special and only within marriage.
- Adultery is wrong and forbidden by the Ten Commandments.

- The Bible shows the importance of sex only happening within marriage to have children.

27. Muslim attitudes to sex outside marriage
1 *Islam*:
- Sex should only take place within marriage.
- Main purpose of sex is to have children.
- Cohabitation is not encouraged.
- Men and women are encouraged to fulfil the desire of sex through marriage.
- Adultery is a sin as it breaks the marriage contract and threatens the family.
2 *Agree*:
- In today's society we have different attitudes towards sex and marriage.
- Not many people follow religious ideas, making them out of date.
- Couples now choose to cohabit so it is unrealistic to expect them to wait.
Disagree:
- The Qur'an teaches that sex should only take place within marriage.
- Adultery is considered a sin in both Christianity and Islam. This includes sex before marriage.
- Muslims do not cohabit because of Islamic teachings about marriage.

28. Christian attitudes to divorce
1 Faithfulness is when a person is loyal and committed to their marriage partner and only has sex with them.
2 *Agree*:
- It breaks the sacrament of marriage made between the couple and God.
- The vows say 'till death us do part'.
- Jesus said divorce was wrong.
Disagree:
- In some cases such as adultery and abuse, divorce may be the lesser of two evils.
- Jesus seemed to suggest divorce was allowed in cases of adultery.
- People can make mistakes and relationships do break down.

29. Muslim attitudes to divorce
1 *Yes*:
- In some cases such as adultery and abuse, divorce may be the lesser of two evils.
- People can make mistakes and relationships do break down.
- The Qur'an allows Muslims to divorce.
No:
- It breaks the sacrament of marriage made between the couple and God.
- Jesus said divorce was wrong.
- Muhammad said divorce was the most hated of lawful things.

2 *Agree*:
- Marriage is a contract in Islam, not a promise to Allah.
- The Qur'an allows Muslims to divorce.
- The family is very important to Muslims and they feel it may be better for children to have divorced parents than to live with hatred and bitterness.
- People can make mistakes and relationships do break down.

Disagree:
- Muhammad, the perfect example, did not divorce.
- Muhammad said divorce was the most hated of lawful things.
- It breaks the sacrament of marriage.
- Divorce shows disrespect to the family.

30. Christian teachings on family life

1 A reconstituted family is where two sets of children become one family when their divorced parents marry each other. They become stepbrothers and stepsisters.

2 • Family is where children are taught about their faith.
- The family is the foundation of society – children are taught right and wrong.
- The Church is seen as a family of Christians.
- Family provides a social environment.
- The Church can support families.

31. Muslim teachings on family life

1 An extended family is when many family members (e.g. parents, children, grandparents, cousins, etc) all live together under one roof.

2 *Yes*:
- Children can be raised within the faith and learn about their religion.
- Beliefs and values can be taught and parents have a great duty and responsibility to raise their children according to their faith.

No:
- Religion doesn't always have a positive influence on children.
- A loving family is all that is required.

32. Christian attitudes to homosexuality

1 *Yes*:
- It is love and commitment that is important not sexual orientation.
- There is nothing wrong with accepting who you are born to be.

No:
- God created man and woman to be together and have children.
- The Bible teaches it is wrong as it threatens society.

2 *Yes*:
- It is love and commitment that is important not sexual orientation.
- There is nothing wrong with accepting who you are born to be.

No:
- God created man and woman to be together and have children.
- The Bible teaches it is wrong as it threatens society and this will always be valid.

33. Muslim attitudes to homosexuality

1 Homosexuality is the attraction of one person to someone from the same sex.

2 *Agree*:
- God created man and woman to be together and have children.
- The Bible teaches it is wrong as it threatens society and this will always be valid.
- Same sex couples cannot have children naturally, which is very important in Islam.
- Homosexuality is banned by the Qur'an and seen as a threat to the stability of society.

Disagree:
- It is love and commitment that is important not sexual orientation.
- There is nothing wrong with accepting who you are born to be.
- Society has moved on and religion should move with it.

34. Christian attitudes to contraception

1 *Agree*:
- It is sensible especially when planning a family.
- It stops the spread of sexually transmitted diseases.
- It may be the right decision to protect the health of the mother.

Disagree:
- Every sexual act should be open to the possibility of a child as this is what God intended.
- God gave a commandment to humans to have children and this is the purpose of marriage.
- Contraception encouraged promiscuity and the spread of diseases.

35. Muslim attitudes to contraception

1 Procreation is making a new life.

2 *Agree*:
- Every sexual act should be open to the possibility of a child as this is what Allah intended.
- God gave a commandment to humans to have children and this is the purpose of marriage.
- Contraception encouraged promiscuity and the spread of diseases.

Disagree:
- It is sensible especially when planning a family.
- It stops the spread of sexually transmitted diseases.
- Muslim authorities allow its use to protect the health of the mother.

36. Key words
1, d; 2, l; 3, c; 4, k; 5, a; 6, b; 7, f; 8, j; 9, g; 10, i; 11, e; 12, h.

Religion and community cohesion

37. Changing attitudes to gender roles in the UK
1 Prejudice is the belief that some people are superior or inferior without getting to know them properly.
2 Discrimination is treating people differently because of their ethnicity, gender, colour or sexuality.
3 *Agree:*
- Men are often still paid more than women.
- In Christianity men and women were seen to have different roles in the past.
- Traditionally men and women are associated with different jobs.

Disagree:
- Men and women have the same rights.
- Men and women can both vote and earn money.
- Men and women may both be involved in the raising of children.

38. Christian attitudes to equal rights for women in religion
1 *Yes:*
- The Bible teaches that men and women were created equally by God.
- There are many examples of men and women being treated equally by Jesus and Christians should follow this example.

No:
- Women are not allowed to become priests within the Roman Catholic Church.
- Women are still traditionally seen as the ones who should stay home and look after the home and children whilst men go out to work and provide.

2 *Support:*
- The Bible teaches that men and women were created equally by God.
- Jesus treated women with great respect.
- Historical evidence of women leaders in the early church.

Don't support:
- Adam was created first and Eve second.
- Traditionally men provided and women stayed at home.
- The teachings of St Paul suggest inequality between men and women.

39. Muslim attitudes to equal rights for women in religion
1 *Islam:*
- Islam teaches men and women are equal and created by God but they have different roles and responsibilities.
- Women do not have to attend the Mosque for prayer.
- A woman's duty is to look after the home and raise the children.
- Muhammad and the prophets were all men.

40. The UK as a multi-ethnic society
1 A multi-ethnic society is where many different cultures and races live together in one society.
2 Racial harmony is where different races live together peacefully and happily.
3 *Yes:*
- People generally do live together and get on peacefully.
- There are benefits such as understanding between people of different races and cultures.

No:
- Many people are worried about the large numbers of ethnic groups coming to live in Britain.
- There have been many examples of conflict and racism.

41. Government action to promote community cohesion
1 *Yes:*
- Organisations such as the Commission for Racial Equality educates the public about these issues.
- The Race Relations Act of 1976 protects people from different races.

No:
- Racism still exists.
- There are many examples of conflict between people from different races today.

2 *Agree:*
- People will always fight and not get on.
- It is difficult to police racism as not all cases are reported.
- There are still many examples of racism today which shows a lack of success (give example).

Disagree:
- There are many examples where government organisations have been successful.
- Protection is put in place for people of different races.

- Relations between people of different races has improved as understanding has grown.
- Christian groups also work to prevent racism such as the Church of England's Race and Community Relationships Committee.

42. Why Christians should promote racial harmony

1
- Christianity is opposed to racism.
- The Bible teaches that all races are equal in the eyes of God as all humans were created equal.
- Jesus always treated all people equally and Christians should try to follow his example.
- Stories such as 'the Parable of the Good Samaritan' teach that we should help others.

2 *Yes*:
- Following the teachings of Christianity means they should.
- Christians should follow the example of people such as Desmond Tutu or Martin Luther King.

No:
- It is everyone's responsibility not just religious believers.
- Everyone deserves equality as they are the same.

43. Why Muslims should promote racial harmony

1 *Agree*:
- Often religion is at the root of conflict.
- Some religious believers think they are better than others.
- You can be racist in spite of your religious teachings.

Disagree:
- The Qur'an teaches that racism is wrong and all people are equal.
- The Qur'an teaches that no race is better than any other and all races are loved by Allah.
- The Church works to help reconcile people.
- The Bible teaches that all people are equal.

44. The UK as a multi-faith society

1 Religious freedom is where people have the right to practice their religion freely and change their religion.

2 *Yes*:
- There will be greater tolerance between people.
- There is better understanding of the beliefs and cultures of others.

No:
- There may be examples of conflict.
- It is difficult for people to adapt to forms of life they are not used to and to be accepted.

3 *Agree*:
- There is greater tolerence between people, including between faiths.

- The Bible teaches that Christians should 'Love thy neighbour'.
- The Qur'an teaches that no race is better than another.

Disagree:
- There are examples of conflict between different religious groups.
- Followers of Islam believe that theirs is the one true religion.
- There can be tensions when people from different faiths marry.
- There can be issues where one group of religious believers tries to convert another to their faith.

45. Issues raised about multi-faith societies

1 Religious pluralism is accepting all religions as having an equal right to co-exist.

2 *Yes*:
- Peer pressure may mean they want to do things which do not agree with their faith.
- Problems raised by interfaith marriages.

No:
- The family and home is where they are taught their traditions.
- They have access to more ideas.

46. Religion and community cohesion

1 *Yes*:
- There is always more that can be done.
- Conflict still exists between some groups.

No:
- They already do so much.
- They try to work together to achieve a common goal.

2
- Heal divisions between faiths through religious groups such as Interfaith Network and Muslim Council of Britain.
- Celebration of festivals and worship to involve more people.
- Encouraging representation of different faith groups in pubic sector jobs such as the police to allow good role models.
- Building strong communities and community links.

47. Issues of religion and community cohesion in the media

1 Racism is the belief that some races are superior to others.

2 *Yes*:
- Storylines on TV show people getting along and living in harmony.
- Documentaries try to develop understanding between different groups.

No:
- The media is out to make money or entertain not necessarily aid community cohesion.

- Often they present a biased view of religious issues and ideas.

48. Key words
1, k; 2, a; 3, g; 4, b; 5, f; 6, h; 7, c; 8, j; 9, d; 10, l; 11, i; 12, e.

Exam skills

49. Exam skills: (a) questions and SPaG
1 Omniscient is a word used to describe God meaning he is all knowing or all seeing.
2 *Yes*:
- There is evidence in holy books such as the Bible.
- There is evidence of God through religious experiences such as miracles.

   No:
- There is no actual proof that God exists. The Bible was not written by him so how do we know that it is true?
- Evidence of evil and suffering suggests that God does not exist because an omni-benevolent and omniscient God would not allow his creation to suffer.

50. Exam skills: (b) questions
Yes:
- Science tells us how the Big Bang started the world.
- We have physical evidence of scientific theories of the creation and development of the world, such as Darwin's theory of evolution.

No:
- Science may explain how the world was created but not why.
- A powerful force must have been necessary to create the universe and only God could be that powerful.
- God caused the Big Bang.

51. Exam skills: (c) questions
1 *Do use*:
- It is sensible for family planning.
- It stops the spread of STI's.
- It may be acceptable if the mother's life or other children may be affected by the birth of another child.
- Sex isn't just about having children – it is also an expression of love and commitment between a couple.

   Don't use:
- It goes against God's teaching that every sexual act should be open to the possibility of children, for example: 'be fruitful and multiply' (Genesis 1:28).
- Christians accept the sanctity of life argument

stating every life is sacred and some forms of contraception are considered similar to abortion.
- Contraception may lead to promiscuity and 'adultery' (including promiscuity) is a sin according to the Ten Commandments.

52. Exam skills: (d) questions
1 *Agree*:
- It is considered a duty for some religious believers, such as some Evangelical Christians, Muslims consider Islam to be the one true religion.
- It allows the message of religion to be spread.
- It is part of religious freedom and in the UK we are entitled to religious freedom.

   Disagree:
- Religion should be chosen, not forced.
- It may be seen as discriminating against those who do not have the same faith as you.
- It can lead to arguments and even violence within a multi-faith society when people are told their religion is wrong.

UNIT 8
Rights and responsibilities

53. Christians and the Bible
1 The Decalogue is the Ten Commandments.
2 *Do*:
- The Bible is the word of God.
- It contains the laws of God.
- It contains the teachings of Jesus.
- The leaders of the Church and their teachings are in it.

   Don't:
- There are better sources of authority such as the conscience or the Church.
- There may be problems with interpretation.
- Some will use a variety of sources for complicated decision.
- It may be considered out of date as it was written so long ago.

54. Christians and the authority of the Church
1 The Church is the community of Christians.
2 *Agree*:
- The conscience may be more reliable as people may hold different views in the Church
- The Bible is the word of God and the most important source of authority.
- The Church's answer may not be the most loving thing to do (Situation Ethics).

   Disagree:
- It helps to talk ideas through with others.
- Church leaders may have more knowledge and experience and be able to give constructive help and advice.

- It offers help and comfort in times of need.

55. Christians and conscience

1
- It is a way of judging the rightness or wrongness of an action.
- Some believe it is the voice of God within.
- St. Paul said you should use your conscience.
- It can be used in any situation.

56. Christians and Situation Ethics

1 Situation Ethics is the idea that Christians should base their moral decisions on what is the most loving thing to do.

2 The Golden Rule is to treat others as you would like to be treated which was a teaching of Jesus.

3 *Yes*:
- It is simple to follow.
- It makes sense to think about how you would like to be treated and is positive.

No:
- What about differences in opinion over how a person wants to be treated?
- It is sometimes difficult to act the way we know we should.

57. Christians and the variety of moral authorities

1 A pressure group is a group formed to influence government policy on a particular issue.

2
- Moral dilemmas are not simple and require many sources of authority.
- They want to make the best decision and therefore this means considering all.
- They want to act the way God wants them to which is contained in many sources.
- An example of an instance where one source may be misleading e.g. The Yorkshire Ripper and conscience.

58. Human rights in the UK

1 *Yes*:
- Humans are more important than anything else.
- All humans were created equally and deserve protection.

No:
- Some humans do not deserve their human rights.
- The survival of our planet should come first.

2 *Agree*:
- All humans were created equal by God.
- All humans deserve protection because they are special and part of God's creation.
- All humans deserve freedom and respect and the essentials of life.

Disagree:
- Some humans such as criminals do not deserve human rights.
- Some people abuse their own or others' human rights.

- Some humans rights and the laws are wrong.

59. Why human rights are important to Christians

1 *Yes*:
- Humans are more important than anything else and their rights must be protected.
- All humans were created equally and deserve protection.

No:
- Some humans do not deserve their human rights.
- Some human rights might be wrong.

2 *Agree*:
- All humans were created by God equally.
- God loves everyone equally.
- The teachings of the Bible are in line with human rights laws, for example, the Golden Rule.

Disagree:
- It is not just up to Christians to fight for people's human rights.
- Some rights in society are not religious.
- Religious rules are more important than human rights laws.

60. The importance of democratic and electoral processes

1 A democratic process is the ways in which citizens can take part in government (usually through elections).

2 A political party is a group that tries to be elected into power on the basis of its policies.

3
- Voting rights were restricted in the past.
- Some people were willing to die to have the right to vote.
- Politics affects every person in the UK.
- The government decides everything that affects people so it is important to have a government that represents the people's interests.
- Voting has power.
- Voting is how change is brought about.

61. Christian teachings on moral duties and responsibilities

1 *Yes*:
- It follows Christian principles.
- It is following the example of Jesus in the Bible.

No:
- Not everyone deserves fair or equal treatment.
- It is difficult to treat someone kindly when they have wronged you.

2
- They believe they should lead their lives according to what God wants.
- They should follow the Ten Commandments.
- They are expected to follow the Golden Rule.

- They are expected to follow the example set by Jesus.

62. The nature of genetic engineering

1 *Good idea*:
- Helps to save life.
- Helps further knowledge.
- Allows us to develop crops and benefit humans.

Not a good idea:
- Nature is complex and we do not understand it fully.
- In the wrong hands these technologies could be dangerous.
- Who makes important decisions in these cases?
- It could lead to other, more serious things, being allowed e.g. designer babies.

2 *Yes*:
- Allows us to advance our medical knowledge.
- May lead to new breakthroughs that could save life.

No:
- We do not know or understand the long term effects.
- Could be dangerous.

63. Christian attitudes to genetic engineering

1 *Good*:
- Helps to save life.
- Helps further knowledge.
- Allows us to develop crops and benefit humans.

Not good:
- Nature is complex and we do not understand it fully.
- In the wrong hands these technologies could be dangerous.
- It could lead to other, more serious things, being allowed e.g. designer babies.

2 *Agree*:
- Helps to save life.
- Helps further knowledge.
- God has given humans knowledge to be able to do this.
- Follows the Golden Rule of treating others the way you would want to be treated.

Disagree:
- Only God can create and take away life.
- Human life is believed to start at conception for some Christians so using embryos and then discarding them is wrong.
- It is wrong to correct defects which do not cause suffering.

64. Key words

1, c; 2, f; 3, i; 4, a; 5, l; 6, d; 7, k; 8, j; 9, b; 10, h; 11, e; 12, g.

Environmental and medical issues

65. Global warming

1 *Yes*:
- We can all individually try to waste less energy.
- The government can help to reduce energy waste and stop global warming.

No:
- If it occurs naturally, we can only do so much.
- Often it involves expensive solutions.

2
- Actions by individuals – reduce energy, be less wasteful, support environmental groups.
- Actions by governments and organisations – putting laws in place, helping the effects.
- Actions by scientists – research more into its causes and solutions.

66. Pollution

1
- Create less waste.
- Government action.
- Use alternative energy sources.
- Use alternative manufacturing methods.

67. Natural resources

1 Conservation is protecting and preserving natural resources and the environment.

2 *Yes*:
- It preserves the earth for future generations.
- It helps to stop the damage we have already done.

No:
- They are often more expensive.
- Some are not available in certain places.

68. Christian teachings on stewardship and attitudes to the environment

1 Stewardship is looking after something so it can be passed on to the next generation.

2 The environment is the surroundings in which plants and animals live and on what they depend to survive.

3 *Agree*:
- The world is also part of God's creation.
- If we do not care for the world, people will not exist.
- God gave humans the duty of stewardship.

Disagree:
- Humans are more important.
- We can help save life which is more valuable.
- It takes more effort to undo the damage done to the environment.

69. Muslim teachings on stewardship and attitudes to the environment

1 *Yes*:
- Religious believers have a duty of stewardship.

- The world is God's creation.

No:
- It should be everyone's responsibility not just religious believers.
- We'll be dead before it has a major impact.

2 *Islam*:
- People should treat the Earth with care as it is Allah's creation.
- Humans were made Khalifahs (stewards).
- Humans have a responsibility to care for the environment.
- All Muslims are part of the ummah which means taking care of the world for future generations.
- Animals are part of God's creation.
- Muslims believe they will be judged in the afterlife on their actions in this life.

70. Medical treatment for infertility

1 An embryo is a fertilised egg in the first eight weeks after conception.
2 In-vitro fertilisation is the method of fertilising a human egg in a test tube.
3 *Agree*:
- It could be used to help people alive now.
- There is no definite success with infertility treatment.
- God has a plan for everyone and this should be respected.

Disagree:
- Every couple has the right to have a child.
- God commanded humans to be fruitful and multiply.
- It is a loving action and follows the Golden Rule of treating others as you would want to be treated.

71. Christian attitudes to fertility treatments

1 *Agree*:
- Everyone has the right to have a child.
- God commanded humans to be fruitful and multiply.
- Jesus told us to 'Love thy neighbour' – giving a couple a child shows love.

Disagree:
- There are other ways to have a child such as adopting.
- It may have little chance of success.
- God has a plan for everyone and this should be respected.

72. Muslim attitudes to fertility treatments

1 *Yes*:
- It is a loving action.
- Every couple deserves the right to have a child.

No:
- There may be religious objections to certain forms of treatment.
- It can be very expensive.

2 *Agree*:
- Infertility is considered a disease so it is okay to try and find a cure.
- Having children is very important in Islam.
- Sperm and egg of the married couple are often used which is acceptable.
- God has given people the ability to create life this way.

Disagree:
- Some believe that if Allah does not want a couple to have a child they should accept it.
- Muslims disagree with the use of donor eggs, donor sperm or surrogacy as they are considered to be the same as adultery.
- People should not play God.

73. Transplant surgery

1 Organ donation is when organs are given to be used in transplant surgery.
2 *Yes*:
- It helps to save lives.
- It is a loving action.

No:
- It should be up to the individual and they should not be forced.
- In Islam, the body and soul are reunited after death so the organs are needed.

3 *Agree*:
- It is a loving action and Jesus taught Christians to 'Love thy neighbour'.
- It saves lives.
- It makes use of organs that would otherwise be wasted.
- There are not enough organ donors.

Disagree:
- It goes against the sanctity of life argument.
- It is interfering with God's plans.
- It can be very expensive.

74. Christian attitudes to transplant surgery

1 *Support*:
- It is a loving and charitable act which fulfils Jesus' teaching to love one another.
- It raises no problems for life after death as the body is not needed in the afterlife.
- It is a way of people showing gratitude for God's gift of life.

Do not support:
- It goes against the sanctity of life argument.
- God created each individual including the organs and it would be wrong to interfere with his creation.
- It interferes with God's plans for each individual.

75. Muslim attitudes to transplant surgery
1 *Agree*:
  • The Muslim Law Council UK supports organ transplantation as a way of stopping pain or saving life.
  • It can save lives.
  • Many Christians believe you don't need your body for resurrection.
  • Golden Rule – treat others as you would want to be treated.

  Disagree:
  • The Qur'an teaches that the body should not be interfered with after death.
  • Muslims believe that the body and soul are reunited in the afterlife and therefore the organs are needed.
  • It goes against the sanctity of life argument.

76. Key words
1, l; 2, e; 3, a; 4, i; 5, j; 6, b; 7, d; 8, k; 9, g; 10, c; 11, h; 12, f.

Peace and conflict

77. Why do wars occur?
1 Aggression is attacking a person without being provoked.
2 Exploitation is taking advantage of a weaker group of people in some way.
3 *Yes*:
  • Sometimes you need to fight in order to achieve peace.
  • Sometimes people need protection which may require fighting.

  No:
  • Peace is never really achieved anyway.
  • War can only bring more pain and suffering.

78. The United Nations (UN) and world peace
1 Conflict resolution is bringing a fight or struggle to a peaceful conclusion.
2 Reconciliation is bringing people together who were opposed to each other.
3 *Yes*:
  • They have been successful in many cases of achieving peace.
  • They have reduced the numbers of weapons.
  • They have organised many peace talks between nations.

  No:
  • We still do not have world peace.
  • Conflicts continue to go on in areas where the UN is involved.

79. Religious organisations and world peace
1 • They encourage reconciliation.

  • They try to educate both sides involved in the conflict.
  • They teach about forgiveness and its importance.
  • They encourage non-violent protest to limit the number of casualties.
  • They speak out against human rights violations.
  • They campaign against governments that appear unjust.
  • They inform the world about conflicts and examples of injustice.
  • Mention examples of organisations such as The World Council of Churches, Pax Christi, Islamic Relief and the Muslim Peace Fellowship.
2 *Yes*:
  • We are working towards this all the time.
  • Organisations help people to talk and discuss their concerns rather than go to conflict.

  No:
  • People and countries will always disagree.
  • Sometimes war and conflict are necessary to achieve the end goal of protecting people.

80. Just war theory
1 *Yes*:
  • There are always valid reasons why wars occur.
  • Self defence.

  No:
  • People use wars for their own gain regardless of the consequences.
  • Both sides may claim a war is just, which is problematic.
2 *Agree*:
  • People are always trying to achieve their own goals in a war.
  • Innocent civilians always die.
  • Both sides may claim theirs is a just war.

  Disagree:
  • If you are fighting to defend your religion e.g. Muslims are expected to fight.
  • War is often a last resort and not wanted but necessary, for example if invaded.
  • If it meets the requirements of Just War theory then it is.

81. Christian attitudes to war
1 Weapons of mass destruction are weapons that can destroy large areas and numbers of people.
2 *Yes*:
  • Some wars are just and therefore necessary.
  • War may be the lesser of two evils in some situations and needed to protect people.

  No:
  • The Bible teaches a message of peace, forgiveness and reconciliation rather than war.
  • Many Christians are pacifists and therefore do not agree with any form of violence.

82. Muslim attitudes to war

1 *Agree*:
  - Many Christians are pacifists and do not agree with any form of violence, Jesus refused to use violence and prevented Peter attacking the soldiers in the garden.
  - The Bible teaches a message of peace, forgiveness and reconciliation rather than war.
  - Peace and reconciliation is at the heart of Islam.
  - Modern warfare means people will always be killed which goes against Islamic principles.
  - Non-violent methods are believed to be the only way to achieve peace.

  Disagree:
  - Some wars are just and therefore necessary.
  - War may be the lesser of two evils in some situations and needed to protect people.
  - The Qur'an teaches it is right if attacked and Muhammad fought in wars.

83. Christian attitudes to bullying

1 Bullying is intimidating or frightening people weaker than yourself.
2 • All bullying involves physical or verbal violence without a just cause which is against Christian teaching.
  - Every person was made in God's image therefore bullying is mistreating God's creation.
  - Jesus taught that people should love one another and treat others as you would like to be treated.
  - Everyone should be treated with respect and weaker people protected.
  - Christians believe they will be judged by God in the afterlife on their actions in this life.

84. Muslim attitudes to bullying

1 Respect is treating a person or their feelings with consideration.
2 *Yes*:
  - No-one should be victimised by bullies.
  - Everyone is equal and deserves to be treated this way with respect.
  - The bullies need help to stop so we need to do more to help them.

  No:
  - Some people need to learn to stand up for themselves.
  - Bullies should be punished not helped.

85. Religious conflict within families

1 *Yes*:
  - Parents may not understand why their child is making certain decisions such as becoming religious or not choosing to be religious.
  - There may be differences of opinions on social issues because society has changed and different generations have different views.

No:
  - There may be other sources of conflict which are just as important.
  - Christianity teaches to 'honour your father and your mother so there should be no conflict'.
2 • A child who converts to another faith or chooses to be an atheists may cause issues.
  - Atheist parents may not know what to do if their child becomes religious.
  - There may be differences in attitudes to social behaviour such as drinking alcohol or sexual issues.
  - Issues such as cohabitation and changes in attitudes over marriage or homosexuality may cause conflict.
  - Choice of boyfriend / girlfriend if they are from a different faith.
  - How children should be raised could causes family conflict.

86. Christian teachings on forgiveness and reconciliation

1 • Christianity teaches that violence is wrong and all conflict should be resolved peacefully.
  - The Bible teaches that forgiveness and reconciliation are the best ways to solve problems.
  - Jesus taught that they were important.
  - Jesus died on the cross to bring forgiveness and reconciliation between God and humanity.

87. Muslim teachings on forgiveness and reconciliation

1 *Yes*:
  - Some actions such as taking the life of another are hard to move on from.
  - Christians argue that if forgiveness means going against a Bible teaching, you should not do it.

  No:
  - Christians should always try to follow the example of Jesus which means forgiving others.
  - It can be difficult to forgive but not impossible.
2 *Disagree*:
  - Some actions cannot be forgotten.
  - It can be difficult to try and forgive if you are the victim.
  - It is difficult to work out where justice lies.

  Agree:
  - The Qur'an teaches that forgiveness and reconciliation are important.
  - Without forgiveness, people cannot move on with their lives as they are bitter.
  - Christians believe they should follow the example of Jesus and try to forgive others.

88. Key words

1, k; 2, g; 3, f; 4, e; 5, a; 6, i; 7, d; 8, b; 9, l; 10, j; 11, h; 12, c.

Crime and punishment

89. The need for law and justice

1 Responsibility means being responsible for your own actions.

2 Justice is the allocation of reward and punishment. it is where people are treated fairly.

3 • People should be rewarded or punished for their actions.
  • Everyone understands justice because it is fairness.
  • Without justice, society would be corrupt and chaotic with people doing what they want.
  • Laws need to be enforced fairly to have order.

90. Theories of punishment

1 Retribution is the idea that punishments should make criminals pay for what they have done wrong.

2 *Yes*:
  • It is a form of punishment and means their freedom is taken away from them.
  • The law is upheld and justice is achieved for the victim of the crime.
  No:
  • Some crimes are more serious than others and therefore need different punishments.
  • Prison is not always effective as some criminals come out and reoffend.

3 *Yes*:
  • Punishment should help the offender to see what they have done wrong and reform.
  • People should be given a second chance.
  No:
  • It just gives criminals more chances.
  • It doesn't work. Nearly half of all criminals reoffend.

91. Christians and justice

1 Judgement is the act of judging people and their actions.

2 • The Bible teaches that God wants humans to act justly.
  • Jesus taught that everyone should be treated equally and fairly.
  • Jesus taught the golden rule of treating others as you would like to be treated.
  • God is just and Christians believe they should act in the same way.
  • All Churches teach that you should behave justly towards others.
  • Christians believe they will be judged after death by God for the way they have acted and behaved in this life.

92. Muslims and justice

1 *Yes*:
  • Religion teaches justice is important so they should always be trying to achieve it.
  • Organisations have more power than individuals in trying to achieve the end aim.
  No:
  • Everyone should be trying to achieve justice in the world not just religious people.
  • If everyone tried to act justly towards others, injustice wouldn't be a problem.

2 *Agree*:
  • Muslims believe justice is important as the Qur'an teaches that God wants people to act this way.
  • Everyone is equal and therefore entitled to be treated this way.
  • Muhammad always acted justly and Muslims should try to follow his example.
  Disagree:
  • They should not put themselves at risk.
  • Sometimes justice is not possible.
  • Everyone should fight for justice and equality, not just religious beliefs.

93. Non-religious arguments about capital punishment

1 Capital punishment is the death penalty where a person is put to death for a crime they committed.

2 *Yes*:
  • It protects society and people.
  • It allows suitable punishment for the criminal and achieves justice.
  No:
  • What if a person is innocent?
  • It can be seen as an easy way out as the criminal does not have to suffer.

3 *Yes*:
  • It would ease the number of people in prisons and protect society.
  • It would show that justice has been given for the most serious crimes.
  No:
  • What if a person is innocent?
  • There are better ways of punishing criminals.

94. Christian attitudes to capital punishment

1 *Agree*:
  • We should give people a chance to reform themselves like Jesus did.
  • It goes against the sanctity of life argument.
  • Jesus taught that revenge was wrong.
  • The overall message of Christianity is love and forgiveness.
  • It can be classed as murder.
  Disagree:
  • Some agree with it for very serious crimes.

- The Old Testament teaches that capital punishment should be used for some crimes.
- Jesus never taught the death penalty was wrong.
- The Church in the Middle Ages used the death penalty.
- Qur'an teaches that capital punishment can be used for some crimes.

95. Muslim attitudes to capital punishment

1 *Support*:
- The Qur'an says that the death penalty can be used for certain crimes.
- Shari'ah says that it can be used for certain crimes.
- Muhammad seemed to agree with the death penalty.
- Muhammad himself sentenced people to death.

Don't support:
- Islamic scholars cannot agree on how the death penalty should be applied.
- The Qur'an only offers capital punishment as an option – it does not have to be used.
- There are strict guidelines given for capital punishment.

96. Drugs and alcohol laws

1 *Yes*:
- In moderation as it may take away the 'forbidden' element.
- This may remove problems such as binge drinking.

No:
- Children are too young to understand the effect of alcohol.
- Children need to be protected.

2 *Agree*:
- There are many cases today of overdosing and addiction.
- The dangers of drugs outweigh any benefits.
- It affects society not just individuals and costs money.
- Bible teaches that God created human bodies and we should not abuse them.
- Qur'an teaches that drugs are forbidden.

Disagree:
- Some drugs are needed for pain relief.
- Some drugs are not as dangerous as others.
- Making them all illegal means people will find new ways of getting them.

97. Social and health problems caused by drugs and alcohol

1
- Excesssive use can lead to addiction. Addicts may turn to crime to fund an expensive addiction.
- Loss of incentive to work due to drug use may lead to unemployment, debt, homelessness.
- Possible social disorder caused by users who are in an altered state of mind.
- Excessive use can lead to health problems such as mental illness, loss of brain function and overdose.
- Addiction can lead to an inability to maintain a regular lifestyle including relationships and family life.

98. Christian attitudes to drugs and alcohol

1
- Drinking alcohol impairs a person's ability to make decisions and changes their behaviour.
- It reduces their ability to act in a Christian way.
- People drank wine in the past because there was no alternative – today we have many types of drinks and alcohol is not needed.
- Alcohol today is much stronger than it was in the past.
- Some Christians believe drinking any alcohol is wrong so avoid it.

99. Muslim attitudes to drugs and alcohol

1 *Yes*:
- It can lead to binge drinking and addiction.
- It can cause social problems for society and leads to illnesses such as liver disease.

No:
- In moderation, it helps people to relax and enjoy themselves.
- Not if taken sensibly.

2 *Yes*:
- Christians use wine in the Eucharist and there are many examples in the Bible but it should be drunk in moderation.
- In moderation, drinking alcohol is acceptable.

No:
- It can lead to different behaviour in people and a lack of control.
- It can have negative consequences such as addiction and health problems.

100. Key words

1, k; 2, a; 3, f; 4, l; 5, h; 6, c; 7, j; 8, e; 9, b; 10, i; 11, d; 12, g.

Exam skills

101. Exam skills: (a) questions and SPaG

1 Forgiveness is when you stop blaming someone and forgive them for something they have done.

2 *Yes*:
- Although there may be different issues in society today, the rules can still be applied and are necessary to ensure a stable society (e.g. murder is always wrong).
- The Ten Commandments were given by God and will always be important.

No:
- Issues and topics have changed for example we live in a multi-faith society and should respect the views of others (you shall have no other gods before me, Remember the Sabbath day).
- People do not follow the Ten Commandments today especially non-religious people.

102. Exam skills: (b) questions

1 *Yes*:
- In order to move on, you have to forgive.
- By following the teachings of Jesus and the Bible, it should be. Jesus taught Christians that 'if you hold anything against anyone, forgive him...' (Mark 11:25).

No:
- Some actions, such as murder, are too evil to be forgiven.
- Some Christians argue that if the conflict was about a religious or moral issue where the Bible had a definite teaching, there can be no reconciliation, for example 'Thou shall not kill'.
- Some actions may not be forgiveable by Muslims, such as working against Islam.

103. Exam skills: (c) questions

1 *Agree*:
- Some Christians believe that God has given us the gift of knowledge and we should use this and technology to help develop and possibly save human life.
- It helps to advance medical knowledge which helps people and follows the teachings of the Bible. Jesus healed people and Christians believe they should follow his example.
- God gave humans dominion over the world. Some Christians believe that as long as it does not cause harm, some forms of genetic engineering, such as GM crops, would be acceptable.
- Jesus taught followers to 'do to others what you would have them do to you'. For some, Christians this could mean that genetic engineering to cure diseases and disorders is acceptable.

Disagree:
- Only God can create life and humans should not 'play God' so some Christians believe that it is therefore wrong.
- It goes against the sanctity of life argument that life is sacred and special and created by God, therefore humans should not be doing anything against this or trying to replicate the work of God.
- Some Christians believe life begins at conception and are opposed to anything that involves research on embryos when some are then discarded.

- We do not know or understand the long-term effects.

104. Exam skills: (d) questions

1 *Agree*:
- God created the planet and gave humans dominion over it. So religious people should look after it. Cars cause pollution and producing pollution is not looking after the planet.
- Religious people should act as stewards for the world and look after the world for future generations, this includes conserving natural resources which are used to run cars.

Disagree:
- Many religious people need cars for work.
- Everybody needs to change their lifestyle to have an impact.
- Religious people have the same rights as everyone else in society.
- New forms of fuel are making cars less environmentally dangerous.

105. Unit 1 Practice exam paper

1 **(a)** Omni-benevolent is the belief that God is all-good or all-loving.

(b) *Yes*:
- If a respected adult tells you something is true, it is likely they will believe it.
- If a child's family holds the same beliefs, they are likely to be influenced by them.
- Within a religious family, belief becomes the norm.

No:
- A child will make up their own mind about belief in God.
- Children cannot be forced to believe anything.
- Teenagers usually rebel against their parents.

(c)
- A miracle is believed to be an act of God that goes against the laws of nature.
- Examples: weeping statue or a person making a full recovery after being told their illness of terminal.
- These may convince non-believers that God is real and acting within the world.
- They may strengthen the faith of believers who have their beliefs about God acting in the world confirmed.
- There are many examples of miracles in the Bible and these could lead to someone accepting that God is real.

(d) *Agree*:
- Best evidence to prove that God is not real as if he was he wouldn't let his creation suffer.
- Humans do not cause natural evil so may question who is responsible.

- It is a powerful argument as it questions both the characteristics and existence of God.

  Disagree:
  - It is possible to accept evil and suffering and still accept God exists as it may be part of God's plan.
  - Many examples of evil and suffering are due to humans and therefore God is not responsible.
  - There are many other explanations where God is not responsible for evil and suffering.

2 **(a)** A miracle is believed to be something that breaks the laws of science and which seems impossible. Religious believers therefore believe only God could have done it.

   (b) *Yes*:
   - They should show religion accurately as they are informing – whether its positive or negative.
   - Sometimes it is appropriate to show religion negatively, for example, extremism.

   No:
   - People may get serious misconceptions if religion is always portrayed negatively.
   - Religion is a controversial topic anyway so this wouldn't help.

   (c)
   - People pray to God in times of trouble wanting help.
   - When prayers are not answered, many may choose to turn away from God or believe that he doesn't exist.
   - People may feel that if a loving God exists, he would care for his creation and answer their prayers.
   - Many people experience pain and suffering in their lives and ask God for help and when this is not given in the way they want, they may choose to reject God.

   (d) *Agree*:
   - The only explanation that makes sense is God as only a powerful force must have created the universe – Thomas Aquina's Cosmological argument.
   - Even if we accept the Big Bang created the world, perhaps God created the Big Bang.
   - The world is so perfect and contains so much that no other explanation makes sense.

   Disagree:
   - Science proves that God did not create the world.
   - The Big Bang and evolution explain everything about our world.
   - There is no physical evidence of God.

3 **(a)** This is the idea that life must have some benefits in order for it to be worth living.

   (b) *Yes*:
   - It may be kinder in cases where the mother has been raped or the child will be born severely disabled.
   - It should always be the mother's choice and therefore an option.

   No:
   - It is the same as murder (taking the life of another) and is always wrong.
   - Life is special and sacred which makes abortion wrong.

   (c) *Islam*:
   - It is taught in the Qur'an, Hadith and Sunnah.
   - It is a key belief in the religion of Islam and important to all Muslims.
   - Heaven is seen to be a reward for being good and Hell is a punishment.
   - It gives meaning and purpose to life.

   (d) *Agree*:
   - The wrong view may be given to people watching.
   - It is wrong to criticise some ideas as extreme.
   - Religious texts such as the Bible and the Qur'an teach Christians and Muslims about matters of life and death and it would offend believers to criticise what their religion tells them.

   Disagree:
   - The media should be allowed to present an accurate view of issues including criticism if necessary.
   - These issues are important and comment will help understanding.
   - The media needs to tackle these issues to show people what they are all about.

4 **(a)** Reincarnation is the belief that after death, souls are reborn into a new body.

   (b) *Yes*:
   - Religion teaches about life after death and the idea we will be judged on our actions in this life.
   - It gives hope that we will again see our loved ones who have died.

   No:
   - There is no physical evidence of any afterlife.
   - We live in a world where science explains everything.

   (c)
   - Sanctity of life argument – life is sacred and special and shouldn't be interfered with.
   - It is viewed as murder as the foetus has the potential to be a person.
   - Humans were created in the image of God meaning life is a gift.

- Every human has the right to life.
- Humans shouldn't play God as only he has this right.
- God has a plan for every human.
- Every life is valued by God even those that may be disabled.

(d) *Agree*:
- The law should be changed to allow people to do the most loving thing, Jesus taught Christians to 'Love thy neighbour'.
- There are people helping others to commit euthanasia today and they are not being prosecuted.
- The law should become tougher so that even life support machines should not be turned off.

Disagree:
- Religious people view life as sacred and so should not take a life – the Bible teaches about the Sanctity of Life.
- Only God should be allowed to take someone's life (Christian and Muslim examples).
- Doctors should keep people alive.

5 (a) Adultery is cheating, when a married person has sex with someone other than their marriage partner.

(b) *Yes*:
- The suffering caused by a couple who no longer love each other staying together may be worse than a divorce.
- Any children should be paramount and if they are being harmed by a marriage, divorce is better.

No:
- Jesus said divorce was wrong.
- Marriage is a sacrament which cannot be broken.

(c) *Islam*:
Allow:
- It is permissible if the mother's life or health would be in danger.
- If existing family might suffer if there was another child, it is more acceptable.

Don't allow:
- Life is a gift from Allah.
- Muslims are expected to have children as family is important.
- Some Muslims are completely opposed to the use of contraception because it is not what was intended by Allah.

(d) *Agree*:
- People can't help if they are born that way.
- Values in society have changed and homosexuality is more acceptable.
- Jesus taught Christians to 'Love thy neighbour', some Christians believe that this applies to homosexuality too.

- It is not illegal.

Disagree:
- Same sex couples cannot have children naturally which is a key belief in Christianity and Islam.
- It is not what God intended.
- Homosexuality is banned by the Qur'an so it would not be acceptable for Muslims to accept homosexuality.

6 (a) Pre-marital sex is sex before marriage.

(b) *Yes*:
- People are still getting married even if they have different types of ceremonies.
- Most people wish to get married and then have children.

No:
- Many people choose to cohabit today rather than get married.
- Marriage is not taken as seriously today and many people choose to get divorced.

(c) *Allow*:
- They are realistic and accept that sometimes marriage doesn't work out.
- It may be the lesser of two evils.
- It is more acceptable in cases of adultery or abuse.

Don't allow:
- Jesus said divorce was wrong.
- Marriage is a sacrament witnessed by God and should not be broken.
- The marriage vows contain 'till death do us part'

(d) *Agree*:
- Children are taught morals and values as they are raised, the Bible teaches children should honour and respect their parents.
- Religion can be passed on to the next generation.
- Family life gives children security and stability.
- In Islam the family is where Muslim values are taught.

Disagree:
- Only having one parent or divorced parents, doesn't mean that children won't be brought up correctly.
- People may rely more on friends than family, which can still provide security, love and good morals.
- In Christianity, the Church is also an important foundation for educating children.

7 (a) Racial harmony is when people from different races live together peacefully.

(b) *Agree*:
- Interfaith marriage can cause problems within religious families.
- People might feel confused by all the different faiths.

- People might try and convert you to their religion.

Disagree:
- People can learn about other faiths.
- A multi-faith society provides opportunities for conversion.
- A multi-faith society allows religious freedom.

(c)
- The government has the duty to ensure that all people are treated equally.
- Without community cohesion there will be division and conflict.
- If the government does not act it could cause social discrimination.
- The government alone has the power to work with different pressure and religious groups.
- The government is able to introduce laws and policies to promote community cohesion.

(d) *Agree*:
- There are many religious teachings against racism, Jesus taught Christians to 'Love thy neighbour' and that all people are created equally, the Qur'an teaches that no race is better than another.
- Religious people should follow their teachings.
- There are many examples of religious people standing up against racism.

Disagree:
- There is still evidence of racism in today's society.
- There is evidence of religious people being racist, e.g. Ku Klux Klan.
- Some religious believers may ignore the teachings of their religion.

8 (a) Discrimination is treating people less favourably because of their ethnicity, gender, colour, sexuality, age or class.

(b) *Yes*:
- They have the power to bring about change through passing laws.
- He government can unite communities and bring people together.

No:
- It is up to every individual to promote community cohesion.
- The government cannot force people to get on together.

(c) *Islam*:
- The Qur'an teaches that Allah made all the races on earth and so Muslims should show people equal respect.
- Muhammad believed all races should be equal and Muslims should follow the example.
- Muhammad said in his last sermon that no one race is superior to any other.

- Muslims believe in one community which promotes racial harmony.

(d) *Agree*:
- Men are still paid more than women in some jobs.
- Muslims believe men and women are different and therefore are treated this way.
- In Catholicism, women cannot be priests.

Disagree:
- Men and women have the same rights in society e.g. to vote.
- Women have been given better status in society.
- Women do have the ability to earn the same as men.

108. Unit 8 Practice exam paper

1 (a) Human rights are the rights and freedoms to which everyone is entitled.

(b) *Yes*:
- It is through voting that people have power and some control.
- Everyone over 18 has this right and should use it.

No:
- Voting doesn't always mean change.
- Many people choose not to vote.

(c)
- They use the teachings of Jesus in the Bible because they believe it is the word of God.
- They use their conscience because they believe it is the voice of God.
- They use situation ethics because they believe it is the best way of following Jesus' command to love your neighbour.
- They take advice from the Church leaders because they are the ones most likely to give the correct advice.
- They use the Ten Commandments because they summarise God's teachings on how to behave.

(d) *Agree*:
- Only God can create life and humans should not play at being God.
- Christians believe life is sacred and special (Sanctity of Life) and should not be interfered with.
- Cloning doesn't save life therefore is not necessary.

Disagree:
- Christians believe God has given them dominion which means power over the world.
- The Golden Rule given by Jesus is to do unto others what you would like done unto you.

- Jesus healed many people and cloning could lead to better medical knowledge.
2 **(a)** A pressure group is a group formed to influence government policy on a given issue.
  (b) *Yes*:
  - Christians have a duty to help others.
  - Christian teachings contains ideas such as helping others and treating others as you would like to be treated.

  No:
  - Everyone should do more not just Christians.
  - The government should do more as they have power and control.

  (c) *Will*:
  - It allows them to follow the Golden Rule.
  - It allows flexibility and the reaction can be appropriate to the situation.
  - It allows them to adapt to a changing society.

  Will not:
  - Church leaders may have more wisdom, so they should be consulted instead.
  - The Bible has absolute authority as the word of God.
  - The most loving thing may lead a person to act against their conscience.

  (d) *Agree*:
  - It was written a long time ago and does not deal with modern problems.
  - It contains rules that are impossible to enforce today.
  - There are many atheists and agnostics for whom it holds no meaning.
  - People of other religions find their own holy books are more relevant.

  Disagree:
  - Examples of how it contains universal laws which will always be important in society (e.g. 'Love thy neighbour', Golden Rule, Ten commandments).
  - The moral teachings of Jesus are a good example to follow.
  - The laws of the country (UK) are based on Christianity.
  - 80% of the population (UK) claim to be Christian.

3 **(a)** Surrogacy is where a woman bears a child on behalf of another woman or where a donated egg is fertilised by the husband's sperm through IVF and implanted into the wife's uterus.
  (b) *Yes*:
  - Pollution causes major problems for the environment.
  - Humans cause a lot of pollution and it is contributing to damage to the environment, climate change and global warming.

No:
- There are other problems such as deforestation.
- Lack of renewable resources is the biggest problem.

(c)
- God gave humans the duty of stewardship which is a God given right to care for the world and environment.
- Humans have a responsibility to care for the world for God.
- God gave humans dominion which means power over the world to care for it and its animals.
- The world is God's creation and hurting it is disrespectful to God.
- The Bible says that God will show anger to those who disrespect his creation.
- Jesus taught about the importance of caring for one another and the world.

(d) *Agree*:
- It is the most loving thing (Golden Rule and Jesus taught Christians to 'Love thy neighbour').
- It can save life which is important.
- Jesus taught that we should help others.

Disagree:
- Islam teaches Muslims that the body and soul will be reunited after death which means the organs are needed.
- The body was created by God and we shouldn't disrespect it.
- Christians believe in the sanctity of life and humans shouldn't play God.

4 **(a)** Global warming is the increase in the temperature of the Earth's atmosphere thought to be caused by the greenhouse effect.
  (b) *Yes*:
  - We all live on the world and therefore should take care of it.
  - Everyone has a responsibility of stewardship given to them by God.

  No:
  - We should just enjoy life and take what we need.
  - The world is there for us to use as we like – we have dominion over it.

  (c) *Will*:
  - God has given humans the capacity to create children through medical treatment.
  - It allows couples to experience the joy of children and is what God intended.
  - It is a way of loving your neighbour and follows the teaching of the Golden Rule.

  Will not:
  - Some may accept it is God's will for them not to have children.

- Some may choose to adopt or do charity work with children.
- Some argue the only way to have a child is naturally through sex which is what God intended.
- Some believe no one has the right to have a child.

(d) *Agree*:
- The problems are too great and one individual cannot achieve anything.
- The world is there for humans to use so we might as well do this.
- Only the government has the power to make a real difference.

Disagree:
- If every person does their bit, collectively we can help.
- There are many organisations and examples of individuals who have helped the environment.
- All Christians have a responsibility of stewardship from God which means we must all (individually and collectively) look after it for future generations.
- Islam teaches that all humans have been given the responsibility of caretaker of the Earth.

5 (a) Pacifism is the belief that all disputes should be settled peacefully.

(b) *Yes*:
- It is the aim of the United Nations who work for this.
- There are examples of successful conflict resolution.
- The goal of all religions is to live in peace.

No:
- People will always conflict over resources.
- People will always conflict over religious ideas.
- Humans are naturally aggressive so there will always be conflict.

(c) *Islam*:
- All Muslims see using violence without a just cause as wrong and sinful.
- All Muslims see humans as a creation of Allah so bullying is mistreating Allah's creation.
- All Muslims teach that it is the duty of religious people to protect the weak and innocent.
- All Muslims believe they will be judged on their actions in this life for the afterlife.

(d) *Agree*:
- The UN peacekeeping forces prevent conflict taking place.
- The UN puts sanctions in to encourage nations to behave properly.

- Religions have contributed to conflict rather than encouraged peace.

Disagree:
- Many conflicts have taken place even with UN intervention.
- Religious groups such as Pax Christi or Islamic Relief do a lot of work to help resolve conflicts.
- Examples of religious teachings on peace and reconciliation, for example, Christianity 'turn the other cheek'.

6 (a) World peace is the ending of war throughout the whole world.

(b) *Yes*:
- Forgiveness is needed to move on – for the victim and the culprit.
- Forgiveness only causes bitterness and a person needs to be able to let go.

No:
- Some actions cannot be forgiven e.g. murder of a loved one.
- Some people do not deserve to be forgiven.

(c) *Islam*:
- Peace and reconciliation is at the heart of Islam (the word Islam means 'peace').
- Modern weapons means innocent civilians will always be killed and injured so this is incompatible with Islamic teachings.
- Non-violent methods are the only way to achieve peace.
- Violence only leads to more violence and was increases hatred between nations and people.

(d) *Agree*:
- Bullies are often victims themselves.
- There are Christian teachings from Jesus about turning the other cheek and loving your enemies however hard this is to do.
- Bullies need help and education to see that what they are doing is wrong.

Disagree:
- If they are not punished or given consequences, they will continue to do it.
- The victims are the ones who deserve sympathy and justice so bullies must be punished.
- If it isn't stopped, it can lead to other forms of evil and violence.

7 (a) Rehabilitation means to restore things to normal life.

(b) *Yes*:
- Punishment can be a deterrent and stop them repeating the action again.
- Punishments can educate people and help them learn that what they did was wrong.

No:
- Many criminals reoffend showing punishment has not helped.
- Some punishments are not severe enough to change a person's behaviour.
- There would be no crime if punishments worked.

(c) *Islam*:
- The Qur'an says Allah is just and humans should be too.
- The Qur'an says that Muslims should treat others fairly as everyone was created equal by Allah.
- Muslims believe they have a role of treating all people fairly given to them by Allah.
- The Shari'ah is based on justice for everyone.

(d) *Agree*:
- Prison doesn't help some and in fact can make them worse.
- Some crimes do not warrant prison initially.
- There is already overcrowding in prisons which doesn't help.
- Some criminals deserve more severe punishments for their crimes.
- It is up to God to judge people and he will forgive those who are truly sorry for what they have done and want to change.

Disagree:
- Criminals should be punished and taking away their freedom is one way.
- It protects society as it takes criminals off the streets.
- Some criminals only learn through punishments like prison.

8 **(a)** Reform is the idea that punishments should try to change criminals so they will not commit crimes again.

(b) *Yes*:
- It should be available for the most severe crimes committed by criminals e.g. murder.
- It brings justice to victims.

No:
- What if a person is innocent and the justice system hasn't worked?
- Capital punishment is the easy way out – criminals needs to be punished by being put in prison to learn that what they did was wrong.

(c) *Do*:
- Some will drink in moderation as the Bible does not forbid the drinking of alcohol.
- Jesus himself drank wine and turned water into wine at a wedding.
- During the Last Supper, Jesus gave the disciples wine.
- Wine is used in the Eucharist and Mass today.

Do not:
- Drinking alcohol can impair a person's judgement and make them act differently.
- There are many other types of non-alcoholic drinks available today.
- Alcohol today is much stronger than in the past and therefore more dangerous.
- Some believe it is better to avoid it as it is disrespectful to God.

(d) *Agree*:
- Punishment is how people learn.
- There are many serious and severe crimes committed today.
- The victim needs justice and society needs protection.
- Christians and Muslims believe justice is important.

Disagree:
- The law is applied in line with the crime committed.
- The punishment can only be given in proportion to the crime.
- What if a person is innocent?
- It is up to God or Allah to judge people and he will forgive those who are truly sorry for what they have done and want to change.

Published by Pearson Education Limited, Edinburgh Gate, Harlow, Essex, CM20 2JE.

www.pearsonschoolsandfecolleges.co.uk

Copies of official specifications for all Edexcel qualifications may be found on the Edexcel wesite: www.edexcel.com

Text © Pearson Education Limited 2012
Edited by Samantha Jackman
Edited and produced by Wearset Ltd, Boldon, Tyne and Wear
Typeset by Jerry Udall
Cover illustration by Miriam Sturdee

The right of Tanya Hill to be identified as author of this work has been asserted by her in accordance with the Copyright, Designs and Patents Act 1988.

First published 2012

16 15
10 9 8 7 6 5 4

British Library Cataloguing in Publication Data
A catalogue record for this book is available from the British Library

ISBN 978 1 446 90528 9

Printed in Slovakia by Neografia

Acknowledgements
Every effort has been made to contact copyright holders of material reproduced in this book. Any omissions will be rectified in subsequent printings if notice is given to the publishers.

In the writing of this book, no Edexcel examiners authored sections relevant to examination papers for which they have responsibility.